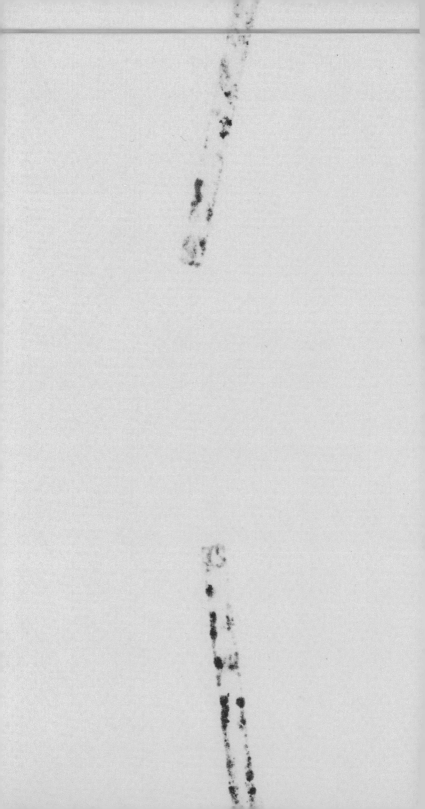

Enabling Acts

Enabling Acts SELECTED
ESSAYS IN CRITICISM

by Louis Coxe

University of Missouri Press
Columbia & London

Copyright © 1976 by   268110
The Curators of the University of Missouri
Library of Congress Catalog Card Number 76–4485
Printed and bound in the United States of America
University of Missouri Press, Columbia, Missouri 65201

Library of Congress Cataloging in Publication Data

Coxe, Louis Osborne, 1918–
    Enabling acts.

    CONTENTS: E. A. Robinson : the lost tradition.—
Beddoes : the mask of parody.—The complex world of James
Gould Cozzens.—What Edith Wharton saw in Innocence. [etc.]
    1. American literature—20th century—History and
criticism—Addresses, essays, lectures. 2. English
literature—19th century—History and criticism—
Addresses, essays, lectures. I. Title.
PS221.C69   820'.9   76–4485
ISBN 0–8262–0200–4

"Edwin Arlington Robinson: The Lost Tradition" first appeared in
the *Sewanee Review* 62 (1954). Copyright 1954 by the University of
the South. Reprinted by permission of the editor.

"Thomas Lovell Beddoes: The Mask of Parody" first appeared in
The Hudson Review 6:2 (Summer 1953).

"The Complex World of James Gould Cozzens" first appeared in
American Literature (1955). Reprinted by permission of Duke University Press.

"What Edith Wharton Saw in Innocence" and "Herman Melville's
The Encantadas" first appeared in *The New Republic*.

"You Never Can Tell: George Bernard Shaw Reviewed" first appeared
in *The Western Humanities Review* 9:4 (Autumn 1955). Reprinted by
permission of *The Western Humanities Review*.

"Romance of the Rose: John Peale Bishop and Phelps Putnam" first
appeared in *The Michigan Quarterly Review* (1974). Reprinted by
permission of *The Michigan Quarterly Review*.

For Allen Tate

Contents

Enabling Acts

Introduction:
A Short View of a Long Matter

The enabling act is change. Beginning with conception, the word grows toward its end, incarnation. Out of the ideal comes the actual. The word is made not symbolic, but symbiotic, flesh.

Metaphor would make the broken whole, whereas images flash and fall, fragments that cannot join. Perhaps in their authentic visualness they may seem to partake more of reality than does the metaphor, yet of themselves they can at best do only what sensibility dictates: show flashes or clusters of a world without connections or relations. Fits of discontinuity raised to a certain power by speed, numbers, and brilliance, images in literature as in motion pictures derive most of their effectiveness from assault, from their way of overwhelming sense and mind. In effect, they make up, out of their close relation with direct physical experience, those "gross stimulants" that Wordsworth saw and foresaw. And yet images or rather imagery must underlie the structure, stand behind the words. It is a matter—perhaps a function—of the relation between sense and soul or imagination.

The aesthetic adventure that is the poem, or work of literary art, makes itself up out of one part genius and two parts reality—the reality that consists in living in a physical world and in continually feeling that world as both plain and fancy, simple and profound, real and ideal. And both poem and poet make each other up as they go along. This is the process of the world-as-metaphor, every man's and woman's act of transferring the sense of the actual world to the realm of spirit and idea and back again—in a continuous performance of the dance of creation.

What can any or all of that mean? To begin with, it may mean that what we need is a good working aesthetic, and by "working" meaning an aesthetic that can help a writer to write and a reader to read. American literature—that body of significance that has had the best title to be called "modern" in the social and psychological senses—has from its beginnings in Poe and Hawthorne and Melville shown that the aim is idea and the feeling of that idea; that the spirit which informs idea can come to us only in the dress and guise of flesh. Americans—those Americans—invented symbolism as a way of thinking, feeling, and—yes—hiding. There are, after all, as Frost once said, "some things that some people aren't fitten to know."

Metaphor in extremis: that seems to be what the most agonized of postromantic literature chiefly demonstrates. Schools of realism, naturalism, even Freudianism and other keys to all mythologies have not been able wholly to kill the lust for metaphor. The lust to conceal precedes the lust to elucidate, to explain away, but what follows does not necessarily exceed or excel. Symbolism comes after romanticism: Hart Crane follows Poe and Melville; Kurt Vonnegut follows Ralph Waldo Emerson. We do not give out the figures on rank in class. What any of us can readily see is that a tradition lives only in the strength of the forebears and the appetite for metaphysical truth in the inheritors.

But the other side of this legend runs further and deeper. Modern literature, American literature, was and is extreme. Our imported writers, if no others, would prove this point, as would a great many of our ordinary citizens. They have come here for those very extremes that America provides. Could Nabokov have written as he has in a lifetime of Switzerland? Did Jerzy Kozinski come here just for Yale and the surfing? If it's raw experience you want and need, for whatever fictional purpose, America should be able to provide it, being itself about the biggest fiction going. It has formed the true subject of most of the best writers, native or adopted, since the renaissance of the early nineteenth century. Why should anyone, let alone a poet or writer of obscure and obscured fictions, want to express, contain, symbolize his country or that part of it which most nearly touches him and his gift? Who needs to go over again all those reasons? Today a writer, or a reader of real writers, may well be more concerned with either a putative inner self or transcendence, as though the American guru of the past had not long since found those matters of Greece and Ionia a bit much and long gone. No, America is not the mystical body of Walt Whitman or Henry Miller, nor is modern literature in America made out of Samuel Beckett and Hermann Hesse. It is made out of the same old home-spun shoddy as before—all that postromantic, postsymbolic irrational self-deception that we have all got used to.

Hart Crane at the end of his poetic rope agonizedly called upon the American Indian, whom Americans had killed, to "lie to us: dance us back our tribal morn." Crane should be alive now to watch the dancers at work and play. He knew it was all a lie, that posturing, that *faux-naif* game, that advertising campaign. America was not West but Waste. The great extremes, dramatics, and grand canyons of the country were all lies. All the time the Whitmans and Emersons, the postromantics and the literary patriots, had been fools of their own lying vision. Melville and Hawthorne were right; Poe knew a haunted palace when he saw one. The true hallmark of the American and postromantic imagination is extremist symbolism. It was the American in Baudelaire who found Poe—an American who could combine symbolism and dandyism. That same composite American becomes Wallace Stevens. And there the strain runs out.

But some genes are recessive. The symbolic imagination may after all have its source not in the accidents of place, person, and time but in the spirit of the language. The trouble with symbolism as practice and aesthetic is that it cheats: it tends to play at irrationality while using rigorous intellectual games as models for poems or stories. It becomes reductive. Starting under the auspices of Imagination, it quickly shifts to Fancy and thence to picture-games. What began in inventiveness turns, by a feat of pure solipsism, into verbal finger painting. That is, what we frequently find in the worst of Hawthorne, as in the worst of Crane and Baudelaire, not to mention Rimbaud, is on the one hand simple associationist stuff, random allusiveness, and on the other hand a schematic system of the writer's own, duly furnished with intellectual credentials to authenticate and dignify the irrational purpose of the poem or story. In the course of this extreme endeavor, language gets lost in words and images. Chaos not only comes again, it becomes both an aesthetic and a purpose. It may in fact be really what Santayana meant by the poetry of Barbarism.

What counts most of all here is the matter of language. Languages live, languages change, languages die. Maybe one or two, like Greek, can put on incorruption, but they have to die first to be born again into that essence. The language of a given time determines the kind of poetry that time will have. When a tradition or a national ethos begins to fail, then the language of the poet asserts itself most strongly. We have all lived off the postromanticism of Tennyson and Yeats while the living language disappeared into the quirkiness of Stevens or Pound—or it went underground. Literature today is not so much debased by the demotic as it is atomized by extreme solipsism on the one hand and frantic derivativeness on the other. The search for new forms, new experience, new poetic "objects" demands encouragement and deserves it sometimes, but it all depends on the hunter and his sense of the country. Happy accidents don't just happen. Unhappy ones do. Baudelaire knew what he had found in Poe, as Eliot knew what in seventeenth century poetry would be good for what ailed him. But Baudelaire already had a language: Eliot did not. He had to make himself over into an ideal Eliot, in a way less dramatic than Yeats's self-renewal, but both ways led to the living language each found fit to his own subject; a language just to the left or right of the common road but there to be found. The real writer, in a time of rapid and total change, must have an acute sense for the language that seems to be made especially for him. Perhaps he merely makes it up and runs the usual risk of obscurity, perversity, and premature death. But he must commit himself somehow to language, because within the close world of the true writer or poet, it is only by language—living words in a vital order—that he can make the metaphors which give life and renewal to the word.

It is necessary to begin somewhere. Endings take care of themselves. By doing one thing, the word becomes another. It takes its rise in a vision of the world apprehended as earth, air, fire, and water, and from that point the word— the language in its best use and life—absorbs the actual as taken in by a perceiving mind, suffers the change of imagining, and becomes both the thing perceived and the perceiving agent. The poet becomes his words, rather than the other way round; his language becomes him. This is not nonsense. It merely recapitulates the old saying, "How do I know what I mean till I see what I say?" Language is the discovery of an event. A poem, in choosing the language it will use, determines how it will write itself and what it will encompass. This allows for accidents as well as calculation: it must give the lie to the old canard of the Greek who tapped his forehead and said that his unwritten tragedy was all done right there in the classical memory bank. If he meant anything at all it was that he had so disciplined himself to the language that the words could be depended upon to write for him, provided he had been and remained faithful to the imagined and imaged action.

It is just here that our contemporary has trouble. Nothing is worth writing about except himself or the impossibility of bringing events and humanity into some kind of, if not causal, then at any rate graspable, relationship. The enormous and incessant assault of the daily news, of the agony of history making itself before his eyes, of the demand that he feel for himself and for those who are not in a position to think or feel: all these simply appall him. It is enough, too much, to show proper indignation. Every poet seems to think himself obligated to turn the general wrong into his own private hell, to see in the fall of a sparrow the vast im-providence of a wicked generation, which of course does not include himself. Or better, his name leads all the rest.

"Short views, for God's sake! Short views!" If the poet or fictionist cannot help feeling and thinking as he does, he can learn another language: metaphor. Transfer all that power from the feeling to the thing felt. Doing by learning. Unmixed media, complex imaginings, short views. We want a poet who sees not life but an image of life steadily and whole—an image of life under stress and in trouble. The image is of war trying to make peace. We honor the soldier because his "trade, verily and essentially, is not slaying but being slain." Love is behind it all, but not as the world gives. Make the image and transfer it to the thing doing and done. Out of that war, that encounter, comes the word, made flesh by the effective transfer of the metaphor from flesh to the word and back again. It is a matter of the diversion of power, the transference of energy. The maker can know his making only in the thing made.

Edwin Arlington Robinson: The Lost Tradition

To the contemporary reader it seems strange that Allen Tate, in 1933, should have referred to E. A. Robinson as the "most famous of living poets" and again as the writer of "some of the finest lyrics of modern times." As far as most of us are concerned, Robinson ekes out a survival in "anthological pickle," as he called it, and few readers try to go beyond, for if any poet has been damned by the anthologists it is Robinson. Why the decline in his reputation? Did critics puff him far beyond his deserts? Can a critic today judge him on the basis of the old chestnuts, "Miniver Cheevy," "Flammonde," "Richard Cory"? Should criticism reiterate that he ruined himself writing those interminable narratives and dismiss him as a "transition figure" between somebody and somebody else, both presumably more "important"? Yvor Winters, in his recent book, has gone far to disestablish the transitional and place the essential Robinson; yet neither he nor Tate has told why he considers the poems he praises praiseworthy. In his brief study, Winters has given an excellent analysis of Robinson's failings and failures, but there is still the problem of the kind of excellence readers who come to Robinson these days should expect. Vicissitudes of temper and fashion apart, I think much of the neglect of Robinson's work has derived from the deceptively old-fashioned appearance it presents and from the very stern cosmology out of which the poetry arises. The texture of the poetry is of a sort we are not used to; the subject matter can be misunderstood. Above all, Robinson's technique lends itself to abuse (and he abused it frequently) so that often the reader may not detect that under an apparently calm surface many forms are in motion.

Robinson is a poet with a prose in view. Read "Eros

Turannos" or "For A Dead Lady" or "The Gift of God"
and you will feel that the scope of a long-naturalistic novel
has emerged from a few stanzas. Yet Tate, in his brief essay,
says that Robinson's lyrics are "dramatic" and that T. S.
Eliot observes this to be a characteristic of the best modern
verse. I really do not know what the word *dramatic* means
in this regard; Robinson's poetry is not dramatic in any
sense of the word commonly accepted, unless it be that
Robinson, like James, likes to unfold a scene. To look for
anything like drama in the poems is idle, in that the excitement they convey is of a muted sort, akin to that which
James himself generates. This poet wears no masks; he is
simply at a distance from his poem, unfolding the "plot,"
letting us see and letting us make what applications we will.
This directness, this prose element, in Robinson's verse is
easy enough to find; less so to define or characterize. One
can say this, however; just as Pope was at his best in a
poetry that had morality and man in society as its subject
matter and its criterion, so Robinson is happiest as a poet
when he starts with a specific human situation or relationship, with a "story." By the same token, he fails most
notably when he engages in philosophic speculation, when
he writes poems, such as the "Octaves," or many of the son-
nets, that have no real subject matter, no focus of events or
crisis seen objectively. The parallel between his method and
that of Pope is patently incomplete, yet each poet, basing
his whole scheme on certain immutable moral convictions
and concerning himself primarily with man as a social creature, strove for a poetry that would be external, transparent, unified. Neither made elaborate experiments with form,
but each was content to exploit with dexterity a few common meters, because for both Pope and Robinson the real
business was what was finally said and communicated. Both
used their individual idioms, each far removed from anything we find today: spare where we are lush, general where
we are specific, detailed where we are reticent or silent. The
twentieth century has learned to dislike abstractions as the

result of being badly cheated by them, yet the fear should perhaps be of the susceptibility to fraud, however pious.

Whatever Robinson's weaknesses, his frauds are few and those few easy to expose. The best poems work toward a condition of total communication by means of suggestion and statement, with no regard for the poet as speaker; that is, the attitudes out of which the poems emerge we take as our own, and there is no need to ascertain those of the speaker, since Robinson is everywhere the same. His irony is not "in" the poem but external, one constituent of a cosmology that sees the human condition as comic in the largest sense—sees life as a desperate business but essentially, immutably unalterable. This is not childish disillusionment; it works out in the poetry as a cosmology that seems to us, scions of the liberal-romantic stock, bitter, profitless, perhaps old-fashioned. And because Robinson so early in his career found and grasped his ultimate beliefs, the modern reader does not find what he must naturally look for: progress, novelty, enlightenment. This poetry does not intend certain things, and discussion of the kind of verse Robinson wrote may clear the ground and allow the reader to go to the poetry with some idea of what not to expect or look for.

Many critics have spent too much time saying that Robinson was obsessed with failure, thereby accounting for his lapse into the profitless slough of the long narratives. Yet none has shown how vital a force the failure is as theme, how it contains within itself a possibility of vision and maturity as well as of pathos. To Robinson life and humanity were failures inasmuch as they consistently fall short of, not the ideal, but their own proper natures. Robinson was never so romantically disillusioned that he could be for long disturbed over the discrepancy between actual and ideal, illusion and reality; for him the real irony, the comedy, lay in man's willful misconception of life and his role in it. The very willfulness may have a magnificence of its own, as in "The Gift of God," and the people in his poems who come through to an awareness of the true proportion do not simply rest there in smug knowledge, but rather for the first time see that it is from such vision of things as they are that a man starts:

> He may by contemplation learn
> A little more than what he knew,
> And even see great oaks return
> To acorns out of which they grew.

What may be irony from one point of view may be comedy or pathos, perhaps a kind of muted tragedy, from another. At all events, the point of view is essentially the same, with only a pace back, forward, or to one side that gives the particular vision its specific color and shape.

The attitudes which have dominated the writing of our century have been rather different from Robinson's. We seem for the most part willing to contemplate life as a tragic affair, to command the ironic tone in our writing in order to express successfully the tragic division we see gaping between what we are and what we would be. Yet one wonders at times if we actually do *believe* this or whether it is another kind of mythmaking, a device for getting poetry written and read, like Yeats's visions. If we really do believe, then we must accept the consequences of our faith; for in a world that is ultimately tragic, happiness is irrelevant, despair the resort of the thin-skinned, and total acceptance the only *modus vivendi*. The acceptance itself must entail a kind of transubstantiation; the Aristotelian essence of life turns to something else while the "accidents" of evil and death remain. This is the realm of miracle, and the poetry of Robinson has nothing to do with it, for his work merely tries to come to a naked vision of the human condition without lusting after schemes of revision, without trying to discover something that is not and can not in nature be there. In "Veteran Sirens" all the terrible irony of mankind's willful refusal to face facts emerges in the pitying portrait of superannuated whores:

> The burning hope, the worn expectancy,
> The martyred humor and the maimed allure,
> Cry out for time to end his levity,
> And age to soften his investiture.

And we are all life's whores. What strikes Robinson as ironic is not the old discrepancy between illusion and reality, not the wastage of time, but the supreme dissipation of the expense of spirit in a waste of shame, folly, and deceit. The stern, still-Calvinist view of carnal sin here has become a trope for life, for the way we all bargain with life for a living and are finally cheated.

The best of Robinson's poems have to do with such plots, such expense of the soul's life, and usually have as their center the single, crucial failure of a man or woman to commit that destruction of the beloved self, to make that complete disavowal of a precious image which alone and finally leaves the individual free. The price of such freedom comes high, "costing not less than everything," and is paid for by a crucial failure in which the image referred to is destroyed, in many such cases along with the life itself. In *Amaranth*, for instance, Atlas and Miss Watchman, both self-deluding artists, are destroyed along with their work; although Fargo, who sees the truth, manages to alter his whole nature and his way of life. The variations on the theme are many. The tone can be somber and tragic, or it can be pastoral and elegiac as in "Isaac and Archibald," or angry and bitter as in "For a Dead Lady." Yet all tones, all attitudes, are part of the one dominating view as the language, however bald or rich by turns it may be, serves the one narrative and ratiocinative end.

If Robinson's attitudes are not common ones, similarly his idiom finds little immediate sympathy in modern readers. Unfortunately we have been accustomed to read Robinson as though he were Edgar Lee Masters from Maine, a crabbed New Englander who should have read Walt Whitman, and unconsciously we judge him by a standard we would reject were it applied to T. S. Eliot or John Crowe Ransom. Here is an old language, reborn, sometimes abstract and involved, usually sparing of metaphor, although the imagery when it occurs is crucial, perhaps the more so because of its very compression and sparseness. Above all, Robinson organizes his poems to a disarming extent, often building a structure that is so symmetrically proportioned that only the closest reading discovers the articulation. Such a reading I shall attempt here in the hope that the effort will supply an insight into the poems themselves as well as a justification of the foregoing remarks.

"Eros Turannos" emerges to the mind as a narrative, compressed and suggestive yet without the trickery that occasionally irritates us, as in the case of "The Whip" or "How Annandale Went Out." Most noticeably, the language is general, the tone expository, the purpose of the poem communication rather than expression. Adumbrated in the first stanza, certain images, whose latent power and meanings are reserved until the final lines, have the function of motifs, repeated constantly and expanded as the poem opens out into suggestion. There are three such images or symbols: waves, tree, stairs leading down. Throughout, these symbols control and provide a center for the meanings possible to the poem, and from the mention of "downward years" and "foamless weirs" in the first stanza to the triple vision of the last four lines these elements recur, the same but altered. As in the case with so many Robinson poems, the reader must supply, from the general materials provided, his own construction, yet the poet has seen to it that there can be only one possible final product. The poem contains two complementary parts: the abstract, generalized statement and the symbolic counterpart of that statement, each constituting a kind of gloss upon the other. Each part moves through the poem parallel to the other, until at the end the two become fused in the concrete images. In addition to the three symbols mentioned, we find also that blindness and dimness, summed up in the single word *veil* yet continually present in the words mask, blurred, dimmed, fades, illusion.

All this culminates in the sweeping final image: "Or like a stairway to the sea / Where down the blind are driven." Yet such inner order, such tight articulation as these examples may indicate, derives no more from the concrete than from the generalized. Contrary to Marianne Moore's professed belief, not all imaginary gardens need have actual toads in them, nor, conversely, do we have to bother with the toad at all if our garden is imagined truly enough. What we must have is room—for toads or nontoads, but room anyhow, and Robinson seems to say that there will be more room if we don't clutter the garden with too many particular sorts of fauna and flora. For in "Eros Turannos" we are not told the where or the wherefore; only, and it is everything, the how and the just so. In the hinted-at complexity of the woman's emotion, in the suggested vagueness of the man's worthlessness, lies the whole history of human trust and self-deception. None shall see this incident for what it really is, and the woman who hides her trouble has as much of the truth as "we" who guess and guess, although the poem implies, coming no nearer to the truth than men usually do.

"Eros Turannos" is the Robinsonian archetype, for in it we can find the basic elements, the structural pattern, that he was to use frequently and with large success. The most cursory reading affords a glimpse into the potential power as well as the dangers of such a form; Robinson's use of it provides examples of both. In the poem in question he reaches an ultimate kind of equipoise of statement and suggestion, generalization and concretion. The first three words of the poem set the tone, provide the key to a "plot" which the rest will set before us. "She fears him": simple statement; what follows will explore the statement, and we shall try to observe the method and evaluate its effect.

> She fears him, and will always ask
>   What fated her to choose him;
> She meets in his engaging mask
>   All reasons to refuse him;
> But what she meets and what she fears

> Are less than are the downward years
> Drawn slowly to the foamless weirs,
>   Of age, were she to lose him.

The epigrammatic tone of the verse strikes one immediately. We are aware that here is a kind of expository writing, capable in its generality of evoking a good deal more than the words state. Important though unobtrusive imagery not only reinforces and enriches the exposition but by calculated ambiguity as well sets a tone of suspense and fatality. The man wears a mask: he conceals something that at once repels and attracts her; notice the play on "engaging" and the implications that involves. The motif is an important one for the poem, as is that contained in the metaphor of "weirs," since these two suggestions of deception, distrust, entrapment, blindness, and decline will be continually alluded to throughout the poem, to find an ultimate range of meaning in the final lines. The second stanza will in such expressions as "blurred" and "to sound" keep us in mind of the motifs mentioned, without actually requiring new imagistic material nor forcing us to reimagine the earlier metaphors. The intent here is not to be vague but to retain in the reader's consciousness what has gone before as that consciousness acquires new impressions. Hence, in stanza three, Robinson can now introduce a suggestive sketch of the man's nature while he reminds of the woman's and continues to explore it:

> A sense of ocean and old trees
>   Envelopes and allures him;
> Tradition, touching all he sees;
>   Beguiles and reassures him;

That engaging mask of his becomes apparent to us here in this man who finds a solace and security in the love of his wife and in her solid place in the community, and yet the sinister note first sounded in the image of "weirs" is lightly alluded to in the phrase "a sense of ocean." Moreover, that

he too is "beguiled" presents a possibility of irony beyond
what has yet been exploited. The stanza extends the narrative beyond what I have indicated:

> And all her doubts of what he says
> Are dimmed with what she knows of days—
> Till even prejudice delays
>   And fades and she secures him.

The possibilities are many. We grasp readily enough the
pathos of her situation: a woman with a worthless husband,
proud and sensitive to what the town is whispering yet
ready to submit to any indignity, to close her eyes and ears,
rather than live alone. Surely a common enough theme in
American writing and one that allows the poet to suggest
rather than dramatize. Again, in "dimmed" we catch an
echo of what has gone before, and in the last two lines the
abstract noun "prejudice," with its deliberately general
verbs "delays" and "fades," presents no image but rather
provokes the imagination to a vision of domestic unhappi-
ness familiar to us all, either in fiction or empirically. And
of course the finality of "secures," ironic neither in itself
nor in its position in the stanza, takes on irony when we
see what such security must be: the woman finds peace only
by blinding herself and by seeing the man as she wishes to
see him.

Stanza four once again recapitulates and explores. Statement alternates with image, the inner suffering with the
world's vision of it:

> And home, where passion lived and died,
> Becomes a place where she can hide,
> While all the town and harbor-side
>   Vibrate with her seclusion.

If this stanza forms the climax of the plot, so to speak, the
next comes to a kind of stasis, the complication of events
and motives and themes we see so often in Henry James.

The outside world of critical townspeople, hinted at before, now comes to the foreground, and we get a complication of attitudes and views—the world's, the woman's, the man's, our own—and the poet's is ours, too. Yet even in a passage as seemingly prosaic and bare as this, Robinson keeps us mindful of what has gone before. In stanza four such words as "falling," "wave," "illusion," "hide," and "harbor" have served to keep us in mind of the various themes as well as to advance the plot, and in the fifth stanza Robinson presents us with a series of possible views of the matter, tells us twice that this is a "story," reiterates that deception and hiding are the main themes, as in the metaphorical expression "veil" as well as in the simple statement, "As if the story of a house / Were told or ever could be." And at last, in the final lines, thematic, narrative, and symbolic materials merge in the three images that accumulate power as they move from the simple to the complex, from the active to the passive, from the less to the more terrible:

> Though like waves breaking it may be,
> Or like a changed familiar tree,
> Or like a stairway to the sea
>   Where down the blind are driven.

For the attentive reader the narrative can not fail. Robinson has given us the suggestive outline we need and told us how, in general, to think about this story. He has kept us constantly aware of place, time, actors, and action even though such awareness is only lightly provoked and not insisted on. In the last stanza the curious downward flow of the poem, the flow of the speculation, reaches an ultimate debouchment—"Where down the blind are driven." Apart from the metrical power, the movement of the poem is significant. Robinson has packed it with words that suggest descent, depth, and removal from sight, so that the terrible acceptance of the notion that we must "take what the god has given" becomes more terrible, more final as it issues out in the logic of statement and imagery and in the logic of the plot.

If much of the poem's power depends upon the interaction of statement and suggestion, still another source of energy is the metric. Robinson here uses a favorite device of his, feminine rhymes, in alternating tetrameter and trimeter lines, and gives to soft-sounding, polysyllabic words important metrical functions. As a result, when he does invert a foot or wrench the rhythm or use a monosyllable, the effect is striking out of all proportion to its apparent surface value. Surely the plucking, sounding quality of the word "vibrate" in the last line of the fourth stanza is proof of this, though equally effective is the position of "down" and "blind" in the final line of the poem.

Contemporary verse has experimented with meters, rhyme, and rhythm to such an extent that one has to attune the ear to Robinson's verse. At first it sounds jingly and mechanical, perhaps inept, but after we make a trial of them, the skill, the calculation, have their way and the occasional deviations from the set pattern take on the greater power because they are derivations:

> Pity, I learned, was not the least
> Of time's offending benefits
> That had now for so long impugned
> The conservation of his wits:
> Rather it was that I should yield,
> Alone, the fealty that presents
> The tribute of a tempered ear
> To an untempered eloquence.

This stanza from "The Wandering Jew" shows the style. This is mastery of prosody; an old-fashioned command of the medium. The reversing of feet, use of alternately polysyllabic and monosyllabic words, of syncopation ("To an untempered eloquence") are devices subtly and sparingly used. The last stanza of the same poem gives another instance, and here the running-on of the sense through three-and-a-half lines adds to the effect:

Whether he still defies or not
The failure of an angry task
That relegates him out of time
To chaos, I can only ask.
But as I knew him, so he was;
And somewhere among men today
Those old, unyielding eyes may flash,
And flinch—and look the other way.

Deviation implies a basic pattern, and although in many cases, particularly in the blank verse narratives, syllable-counting mars the prosody, nonetheless the best poems subtly attune themselves to the "tempered ear," syncopate on occasion, and jingle to good effect.

This analysis is technical and only partial; it seems to presuppose that we must lapse into Mr. Brooks's "heresy of paraphrase." Granted. Yet this but begs a question, inasmuch as all of Robinson's poetry assumes that one will want to find the paraphrasable element the poet has carefully provided. These are poems about something, and what the something is we must discover. That is why we should consider Robinson as a poet with a prose in view, according to the description of *prose* earlier suggested. "Eros Turannos" is about the marriage of untrue minds, but specifically it is not about just untrueness and minds; it is about untrue man A and suffering, self-deluding woman B, as well as about those worldly wise men who conjecture and have all the dope. Notably unsuccessful in speculative verse, Robinson excels in just this naturalistic case history, this story of a Maine Emma Bovary. If the theme is still failure, Robinson rings a peculiar change upon it, since at last the poem forces us to accept the implication that there is and must be a "kindly veil between / Her visions and those we have seen"; that all of us must "take what the god has given," for failure is, in Robinson's world, the condition of man and human life. We do the best we can. In "Old Trails," the best one can is not often good, and what is indeed success in the world's eyes has a very shoddy look to those who recognize the success as merely "a safer way / Than growing old alone among the ghosts." It is the success of Chad in *The Ambassadors*, who will go home to the prosperous mills and Mamie and Mom, not that of Strether, who could have had the money and the ease but took the way of "growing old among the ghosts." But a briefer, more compact poem than "Old Trails," one that deals with another aspect of the theme, is the sonnet "The Clerks," which for all its seeming spareness is a very rich, very deft performance.

The octave opens colloquially, gives us a general location and an unspecified number of clerks; the speaker is the poet, as poet and as man. Robinson draws an evocative, generalized sketch of the clerks' past, of their prime as well as of the slow attrition of time and labor, and affirms that despite the wear they have sustained these men are still good and human. It is in the sestet that the poem moves out into suggestion, that it implies a conceit by which we can see how all men are clerks, timeservers, who are subject to fears and visions, who are high and low, and who as they tier up also cut down the trim away. To call the poem a conceit is no mere exercise of wit, for Robinson has clearly punned on many unobtrusive words in the sonnet. What is the clerks' "ancient air"? Does it mean simply that the men are old and tired, or that their manner is one of recalling grand old times of companionship that never really existed, or that one must take "air" literally to mean their musty smell of the store? These possibilities are rendered the more complex by the phrase "shopworn brotherhood" immediately following, for then the visual element is reinforced, the atmosphere of shoddiness and shabbiness, of Rotary-club good-fellowship, and the simple language has invested itself with imagistic material that is both olfactory and visual. And of course, one may well suspect sarcasm in the assertion that "the men were just as good, / And just as human as they ever were." How good were they? Yet lest anyone feel this is too cynical, Robinson carefully equates the clerks with "poets and kings."

As is the case with "Eros Turannos," this poem proceeds from the general to the specific and back to the general again, a generality now enlarged to include comment
on and a kind of definition of the human condition. Throughout, there have been ironic overtones, ironic according to
the irony we have seen as peculiarly Robinsonian in that it
forms one quadrant of the total view. Here, the irony has to
do with the discrepancy between the vision men have of
their lives and the actuality they have lived. The poet here
implies that such discrepancy, such imperfection of vision
is immutably "human" and perhaps, therefore and ironically, "good." That the clerks (and we are all clerks) see themselves as at once changed and the same, "fair" yet only
called so, serves as the kind of lie men exist by, a lie that
becomes an "ache" on the one hand and the very nutriment
that supports life on the other. You, all you who secretly
cherish some irrational hope or comfort, you merely "feed
yourselves with your descent," your ancestry, your career,
your abject position miscalled a progress. For all of us there
can be only the wastage, the building up to the point of dis-
satisfaction, the clipping away to the point of despair.

Despite the almost insupportable duress of Robinson's
attitude, we can hardly accuse him of cynicism or hopeless-
ness. In every instance his view of people is warm and understanding, not as the patronizing seer but as the fellow
sufferer. Such feeling informs the poems we have discussed
and fills "The Gift of God" with humanity no cynic could
imagine, no despair encompass. For in this poem the theme
of failure turns once more, this time in an unexpected way
so that we see Robinson affirming self-deception of this
specific kind as more human, more the gauge of true love
than all the snide fact-finding the rest of the world would
recommend. The poem is about a mother's stubborn, blind
love for a worthless (or perhaps merely ordinary) son, and
this in the teeth of all the evidence her neighbors would be
delighted to retail. Again, the poem is a compact narrative;
again the irony exists outside the poem, not in its expres-

sion. As in so many of the best poems, Robinson says in effect: here is the reality, here is the illusion. *You* compare them and say which is which and if possible which is the correct moral choice.

The metaphorical material we can roughly classify as made up of imagery relating to royalty, apotheosis, sacrifice, and love. From the first few lines we are aware of a quality which, by allusion to the Annunciation and the anointing of kings, establishes the mother's cherished illusion and thereby makes acceptance of the emergent irony inescapably the reader's duty. He must compare the fact and the fiction for and by himself; Robinson will not say anything in such a way as to make the responsibility for choice his own rather than the reader's. He will simply render the situation and leave us to judge it, for all of Robinson's poems presuppose an outside world of critics and judges, of ourselves, people who see and observe more or less clearly. His irony is external; it lies in the always hinted-at conflict between the public life and the private, between the thing seen from the inside and from the outside; with the poet as a speaker presenting a third vision, not one that reconciles or cancels the other two, but one which simply adds a dimension and shows us that "everything is true in a different sense."

If the dominant motifs in "The Gift of God" are as indicated above, the progression of the poem follows undeviatingly the pattern suggested. In the first stanza Annunciation; the second, Nativity; the third, vision; the fourth, a stasis in which the mother seems to accept her son's unusual merit and her own vision of him as real; the fifth, a further extension of vision beyond anything actual; the sixth, the culmination of this calculated vision in the apotheosis. More than a schematized structure, the poem depends not only on the articulation of motifs and a plot but equally on symbolic material that interacts with the stated or implied events in the "plot." Thus, from the outset the poet has juxtaposed the illusory vision and the "firmness" of the mother's faith in it. The language has a flavor of vague association with kingship, biblical story, and legend, notably conveyed by such words as "shining," "degree," "anointed," "sacrilege," "transmutes," and "crowns." Yet in the careful arrangement of his poem Robinson has not oversimplified the mother's attitude. She maintains her "innocence unwrung" (and the irony of the allusion is not insisted upon) despite the common knowledge of people who know, of course, better, and Robinson more than implies the innocence of her love in the elevated yet unmetaphorical diction he uses. Not until the final stanza does he open the poem, suddenly show the apotheosis in the image of "roses thrown on marble stairs," subtly compressing into the last three lines the total pathos of the poem, for the son ascending in the mother's dream is "clouded" by a "fall"; the greatness his mother envisions is belied by what we see. And who is in the right? For in the final turn of the plot, is it not the mother who gives the roses of love and the marble of enduring faith? Is the dream not as solid and as real as human love can make it? If we doubt this notion, we need only observe the value Robinson places on the verb *transmutes* in stanza five: "Transmutes him with her faith and praise." She has, by an absolute miracle of alchemy, transmuted base material into precious; by an act of faith, however misplaced, she has found the philosopher's stone, which is love wholly purged of self. What we have come to realize is that, in these poems we have been considering, we are concerned with narrative —narrative of a peculiar kind in which the story is not just about the events, people, and relationships but about those very poetic devices which are the vehicle of the narration and its insights. In "The Gift of God" symbol and theme have a narrative function; they must do in brief and without obtrusiveness what long passages of dialogue, exposition, and description would effect in a novel. As a result, the reader is compelled to take the entire poem in at once; he either "understands" it or he does not. Naturally there are subtleties that emerge only after many readings; yet because these poems are narratives, Robinson must concentrate upon communication, upon giving us a surface that is at once dense yet readily available to the understanding.

> As one apart, immune, alone,
> Or featured for the shining ones,
> And like to none that she has known
> Of other women's other sons,
> The firm fruition of her need,
> He shines anointed; and he blurs
> Her vision, till it seems indeed
> A sacrilege to call him hers.

This is on one hand a simple telling of the plot: the mother sees her son as unique and feels unworthy to be his mother. Simple enough. But the story is more than this, more than a cold telling of the facts about the mother's vision of her son. We see on the other hand that it is her need of the son, and of the vision of him, which complicates the story, while the suggestion of kingship, ritual, and sacrifice in the diction, the implication of self-immolation and deception, further extends the possibilities of meaning. All this we grasp more readily than we may realize, for Robinson prepares for his effects very early; and while he extends meaning is careful to recapitulate, to restate and reemphasize the while he varies and complicates:

> She sees him rather at the goal,
> Still shining; and her dream foretells
> The proper shining of a soul
> Where nothing ordinary dwells.

In these lines Robinson affirms the mother's illusion: it is a "dream" that "foretells," and recapitulates the theme of kingship, of near divinity in the repetition of "shining." The stanza that follows gives the poem its turn, states specifically that the son is merely ordinary, that the mother deludes herself, that her motive in so doing is "innocent," and in

stanza five the poem, as we have seen, turns once more,
pivots on the verb "transmute," turns away from the simple
ironical comparison we have been experiencing, and reveals
a transmuted relationship: son to mother, vision to fact, and
an ultimate apotheosis of the mother under the guise of a
mistaken view of the son. The poem is about all these things
and is equally about the means of their accomplishment
within the poem. This is a poetry of surfaces, dense and
deceptive surfaces to be sure but none the less a poetry that
insists upon the communication of a whole meaning, totally
and at once:

> She crowns him with her gratefulness,
> And says again that life is good;
> And should the gift of God be less
> In him than in her motherhood,
> His fame, though vague, will not be small,
> As upward through her dream he fares,
>
> Half clouded with a crimson fall
> Of roses thrown on marble stairs.

The recapitulation, the tying together, of the symbolic and
thematic materials serves in this, the last stanza, a narrative
as well as an expressive purpose. The tone is epigrammatic
rather than prosaic and must shift delicately, come to the
edge of banality, then turn off and finally achieve a muted
sublimity that runs every risk of sentimentality and rhetoric
yet never falters. The verse requires of us what it requires
of itself: a toughness that can encompass the trite and
mawkish without on the one hand turning sentimental itself
or on the other resorting to an easy irony. The technique is
the opposite of dramatic in that Robinson leaves as much to
the reader as he possibly can; he uses no persona; the conflict is given not so much as conflict-in-action before our
eyes as it unfolds itself at once, passes through complications, and returns to the starting point, the same yet altered
and, to some degree, understood. To this extent Robinson

is ratiocinative rather than dramatic. What we and the characters themselves think about the "plot" is as important as the plot, becomes indeed the full meaning of the plot.

Observably this ratiocinative and narrative strain tends toward a kind of self-parody or formula. Robinson resorted to trickery too often in default of a really felt subject matter, as in "The Whip." Yet we must not feel that between the excellence of such poems as "For A Dead Lady" and the dullness of *King Jasper* there lies only a horde of mediocre poems; on the contrary, there is no American poet who has approached Robinson in the number of finished poems of high merit. Winters's list seems to me an excellent one, though it may seem overly strict to some. In any case, it clearly indicates that Robinson is *the* major American poet of our era, with only T. S. Eliot as a peer. Of possible rivals, there is none whose claim rests on the number of *finished* poems nor on wholly achieved effects nor on the range and viability of subject. Of course, this is a controversial state-ment in many quarters, and odious comparisons are far from the purpose; nevertheless, until such time as serious readers of serious poetry make an attempt to read and evalu-ate Robinson's poetry, they must take somebody else's word for it. The poetry is there—a fat volume with all the arid narratives at the end for convenience, the better poems scattered throughout. It may be that the time has come for readers of poetry to place Robinson where he belongs, or to read him at any rate. I have attempted to reveal some of the more striking virtues of the poetry and to dispel some misconceptions, and while I suppose there are readers who do not like Robinson's *kind* of poetry, I have tried to show what we must not look for in it. It is to me important to get beyond fashion if we can and take stock of our best writers, not being deterred by what we have been trained to think about them nor discouraged by faults that loom large to us because they are not our own. If we can understand if not believe in his external irony, his cosmology, then we shall be equipped to recognize his worth in the same way that we recognize that of Swift, for example, or Mauriac. Time and fashion will have their effects, true enough, but unless we can rise above the predilections of the moment in our reading, there is little possibility of our understanding what we read.

Thomas Lovell Beddoes:
The Mask of Parody

The poetry of Thomas Lovell Beddoes should find in our time a place denied it in its own if only because we are today interested in deviation for its own sake. Beddoes's life, curious and expatriate, a life that shows him as radical, scientist, psychiatric case, and necrophile, alone would attract our age. The poetry, however, is the subject here, and it is a poetry of a sort that seems to me to offer a way out for the modern writer while it exists in its own world as a strange, viable creation.

Beddoes wished to be a dramatist. His major work, *Death's Jest-Book*, shows at once the limitations, potentialities, and achieved merits of his dramatic verse. Its texture derives from morality and symbol, from poetic language, and these are the vehicles of the drama as exciting theater. A packed, metaphorical idiom, bristling with allusion and learning, a boisterous humor that moves deliberately into the grotesque, a sense of terror before the omnipresence of death: such is the element of the extraordinary play in the composition of which Beddoes spent the most productive years of his life.

"To have my way, in spite of your tongue and reason's teeth, tastes better than Hungary wine; and my heart beats in a honeypot now I reject you and all sober sense." So speaks Mandrake, the disciple of Paracelsus, but it might well be Beddoes himself. Yet it was not in a "dérèglement de tous les sens" that he sought a freedom, but in an elusive grand synthesis of search in which he raided the culture, artistic and scientific, of the West. His poetry clearly reflects this search. From Hebrew lore to contemporary anatomy, from Pythagoras to Shelley, he roves back and forth through history, and the poetry is dense with references, literary and scientific, which reinforce and accentuate a genuine originality. *Death's Jest-Book* may at times become pastiche on the one hand and chaos on the other. Brought up on a diet of the Elizabethan and Jacobean playwrights, Beddoes, like all of his contemporaries who tried "dramaturgy," never got free of the influence. Yet in this instance it is a happy fault, for no other of the romantic playwrights caught the idiom they echoed as fully as he did, and none had the sense of drama in the very feel of the verse to anything like the extent notable in the best parts of *Death's Jest-Book*.

The play's plot is, "God save us, a thing of naught," or rather, of a great deal too much, most of it confused. The satanic jester, Isbrand, usurps Melveric's dukedom—partly in vengeance for Melveric's murder of Isbrand's father and his brother, Wolfram. As the plot to seize the duchy of Grussau culminates, Isbrand is betrayed and killed, Melveric drawn living into the grave, various other characters are variously slain. There is a subplot providing love interest, but plot is not the issue here.

To call such a congeries of implausibilities absurd is only proper; the action is eccentric; one cannot find a tragic hero or a single conflict. Beddoes alters his scheme and his intent more than once; the subplotting is at best irrelevant and at worst confusing as well as dull. The dramatic and poetic excitement resides in the byplay, and that for the most part concerns Isbrand, the demonic fool of Death, in whose actions and speeches we can find the essence of Beddoes's poetic gift and an adumbration at least of a form of tragedy.

Here excess is the key. Excess, calculated or at times merely chaotic, crowds into action, structure, and metaphor. It is in this respect above all that Beddoes is a poet worthy of our attention, for he did not fear a risk, in particular that most dangerous of all risks: being caught in a generalization or a cliché. And perhaps because he was remote from his contemporaries, because he was unafraid of traditional, stock situations, his best dramatic verse is exciting in language, metaphor, and movement. He had grasped what too few dramatists today believe, that the vehicle of a play is not character but language, a particular language that is theatrical in that it conveys the immediate action while it points ahead to impending tragedy. Consider this passage, in which Isbrand converses with one of his henchmen over the body of the treacherously slain Wolfram.

> ISBRAND: . . . This was one who would be constant in friendship and the pole wanders: one who would be immortal, and the light that shines upon his pale forehead now, through yonder gewgaw window, undulated from its star hundreds of years ago. That is constancy, that is life. O mortal nature!
>
> SIEGFRIED: 'Tis well that you are reconciled to his lot and your own.
>
> ISBRAND: Reconciled! A word out of a love tale, that's not in my language. No, no. I am patient and still and laborious, a good contented man; peaceable as an ass chewing a thistle; and my thistle is revenge. I do but whisper it now: but hereafter I will thunder the word, and I shall shoot up gigantic out of this pismire shape, and hurl the bolt of that revenge.

The modern obsession with personality concerns Beddoes little. Somehow he knew that character as such is one thing in life and quite another in art, in the drama. In either case seeing a man as a mere agglomeration of motives or qualities is little help and no explanation. Since in a play what interests the spectator is the thing done, the way it is done, and its effect on people or on further action, the establishing of character is merely one way of making an action seem credible or interesting. In the romantic period, one that was curious about emotion, morality, and ideas, *character* of an intricate sort had little function in drama, for there was more than enough character available in actual life. In our day, when symbol and thing symbolized have split apart, *personality* has triumphed, with psychiatric quirks the stuff of drama and life alike. Beddoes, indif-

ferent to this concern, instinctively returned to something
like a doctrine of humors, of ruling passions, since his mind
increasingly reached out for absolutes: the meaning of
death, the vanity of human wishes, the nature of human
freedom. What better convention, what more fascinating
ritual, could he have chosen than the old revenge tragedy,
with all its layers of association, its formal appeal to the
spectators' powers of suspending disbelief, its open invitation to rhetoric and excess? We must not look to *Death's
Jest-Book* for originality of motive or plot. If there is a
particular view of the action it would appear to be a double
one. We are to see the events as deviations from a norm
of moral behavior and consequently to condemn them, but
we are not to empathize automatically. One part of the mind
must be reserved to participate in the poetic and dramatic
processes, to judge of what allows one to be moved, and
simultaneously to say, "That was a fine touch."

What is new about this? It is so old that a revival of
the attitude in the theater today would create an effect of
extreme novelty that no experiment with gadgetry could
rival. Beddoes found in the Jacobean drama certain habits
of mind that corresponded to his own:

> ISBRAND: . . . Isbrand, thou tragic fool,
> Cheer up. Art thou alone? Why so should be
> Creators and destroyers. I'll go brood,
> And strain my burning and distracted soul
> Against the naked spirit of the world
> Till some portent's begotten.

Beddoes, unlike his Isbrand, knows that man is less than
angel, and indeed at the end of the play Isbrand has well
earned his cap and bells. "For now indeed Death makes a
fool of me," he says as he dies. And this was the same Isbrand who had earlier defied the universe:

> I have a bit of FIAT in my soul,
> And can myself create my little world.
> Had I been born a four-legged child, methinks

I might have found the steps from dog to man,
And crept into his nature. Are there not
Those that fall down out of humanity,
Into the story where the four-legged dwell?

The lesson we can learn from Beddoes may go something like this: it is all a risk, this writing poetry and plays. Yet if art is going to be different enough from life to be worth bothering about, then make that difference exciting, excessive, bold. Poetry must reassemble the bones of the language and recreate "the bloody, soul-possessed weed called man," quickened out of sheer art, sheer creation.

But of course Beddoes is no playable dramatist. How stage the impossible slaughters, poisonings, tilts, and apparitions? Perhaps there is no physical bar, but other more serious obstacles would confront the director. Beddoes had no stagecraft and knew nothing at all about the theater. His head full of Schiller and Goethe's *Götz von Berlichingen*, of ideas about the stage that would make a modern producer shudder. And with reason. However promising the work of the inexperienced playwright may prove, it is only that. Beddoes had no chance to use a stage or to see his work performed; how could he have learned? Yet despite this, he had an attribute that is equally indispensable: he knew that language can be dramatic of itself and was able to make it so. No small measure of his success with dramatic language comes from his preoccupation with extremes, of subject and of expression. At times this becomes almost surrealist (if I understand the term), the driving to an extreme of fancy a conceit or an insight:

> ISBRAND: . . . One has said, that time
> Is a great river running to eternity.
> Methinks 'tis all one water, and the fragments,
> That crumble off our ever dwindling life,
> Dropping into't, first make the twelve-houred circle,
> And that spreads outward to the great round Ever.
> THORWALD: You're fanciful.
> ISBRAND: A very ballad-maker.

There is often sarcasm or perhaps contempt in Isbrand's tone. He shares with the diabolic figures of much romantic verse a mocking attitude; like Goethe's Mephistopheles he has the "denying spirit," though it is certainly not as objectively expressed. Yet he also shares some of the qualities of the Shakespearean fool, since his wisdom continually clashes with the nonsense of Everyman. The vengeance Isbrand seeks, the power he would usurp, becomes under Beddoes's hand generalized, as though the Duke and his Grussau are mere surrogates for a contempt Isbrand (and Beddoes) feels for humanity: "As I live I grow ashamed of the duality of my legs, for they and the apparel, forked or furbelowed, upon them constitute humanity; the brain no longer; and I wish I were an honest fellow of four shins when I look into the notebook of your absurdities. I will abdicate." Isbrand is the intellectual who scorns the court, the world of mediocrity; yet maladjusted as he may be, there is no self-pity in him. "How I despise all such mere men of muscle," he says, and proceeds with his plan to seize the dukedom. If the world will not conform to his desire, he will force it, by the power of his intellect, to serve him. No irony here, save what eventuates in dramatic irony; Isbrand is deadly serious, committed to a program that entails convulsions in the state. This intellectual, this eccentric of many masks and desires, will get beyond human weakness if he die for it; and this is true of Beddoes's writing of the role. Isbrand, when in his more playful mood, resorts to the grotesque, to a species of surrealism as the lighter expression of a demonic will. He is conscious that he is at court, "and there it were a sin to call anything by its right name." Though he "abdicates," ceases formally to be a jester, yet the role of poet is ready for him, another mask that he may wear until the plot is ripe and he may put off disguises. We can often identify Beddoes with Isbrand if only because the surrealist tone of much of the poetry in *Death's Jest-Book* derives from the dominant attitudes of Beddoes himself, from his recondite learning, his necrophilia, his passion for an all-containing synthesis. The grotesque element in the poetry is mask—the playful aspect, at times grim, behind which Beddoes hides his contempt for man as he is, his yearning for another form more suited to man's will to change and grow. Hence death is welcome, for ultimately it may mean rebirth, a new and more appropriate form. Poetry, then, should distort life and all normal views of it. That is what Isbrand does when he wears the mask of poet. It is Beddoes's mask too, and both their tragedies; to make man over is impossible, yet the unusual man must try. Tragedy comes from that trial. Poetry comes from expressing it. A poetic tragedy is an excessive showing of excess.

If Beddoes's idea of tragedy seems inadequate, too far removed from the possibility of alternatives, too personal, it is at least modern, an idea that should find sympathetic consideration today. Isbrand, as he is dying, understands that he "in a wicked masque would play the Devil" and that there can be ruin only for such a player. The diabolism strikes home. Isbrand further says: "But jealous Lucifer himself appeared / And bore him—whither? I shall know tomorrow." If there is to be real tragedy, a man must know in advance the risks he takes; both Beddoes and Isbrand see risks in the ways taken, but they do not know for sure the nature of the risks. They will "know tomorrow." In the faint of heart, such uncertainty leads to scepticism, to irony, to the disillusionment of the sophisticated child. In those strong enough to face the bitterness of *wanhope*, there is this resort: gesture, mask, and finally, parody. We can find a full expression of this in one of the play's songs, a curious piece of work that revolted Beddoes's friend Barry Cornwall and is of one temper with the unease conveyed to Browning, who would neither release nor reread the Beddoes manuscripts entrusted to him. This song shows us what Beddoes was after, shows us perhaps why no tragedy could ever contain it.

"What is the lobster's tune while he is boiling?" asks

Isbrand, and begins his song. Whether one looks at the
poem as a mere burlesque or as a whole genre by itself,
there is still this question: how does critic or reader deal
with such a work? For if we can call this irony, the word has
finally lost any real meaning, and if we dismiss it as fanciful, grotesque, or Freudian we miss the point, a point we
would do well to seize.

Song by ISBRAND

Squats on a toadstool under a tree
A bodiless childfull of life in the gloom,
Crying with frog voice, "What shall I be?"
Poor unborn ghost, for my mother killed me
Scarcely alive in her wicked womb.
What shall I be? Shall I creep to the egg
That's cracking asunder yonder by Nile,
      And with eighteen toes
      And a snuff-taking nose,
Make an Egyptian crocodile?
Sing, "Catch a mummy by the leg
      And crunch him with an upper jaw,
      Wagging tail and clenching claw;
      Take a bill-full from my craw,
      Neighbor raven, caw, o caw,
      Grunt, my crocky, pretty maw!
         And give a paw."

Swine, shall I be you? Thou art a dear dog;
But for a smile, and kiss, and pout,
I much prefer *your* black-lipped snout,
      Little, gruntless, fairy hog,
      Godson of the hawthorn hedge.
For, when Ringwood snuffs me out,
And 'gins my tender paunch to grapple,
Sing, " 'Twixt your ancles visage wedge
      And roll up like an apple."

Serpent Lucifer, how do you do?
Of your worms and your snakes I'd be one or two;
      For in this dear planet of wool and of leather

'Tis pleasant to need neither shirt, sleeve, nor shoe,
    And have arm, leg, and belly together.
    Then aches your head, or are you lazy?
    Sing, "Round your neck your belly wrap,
    Tail atop, and make your cap
        Any bee and daisy."

I'll not be a fool like the nightingale
Who sits up all midnight without any ale,
    Making a noise with his nose:
Nor a camel, although 'tis a beautiful back;
Nor a duck, notwithstanding the music of quack
    And the webby, mud-patting toes.
I'll be a new bird, with the head of an ass,
Two pigs' feet, two men's feet, and two of a hen;
Devil-winged; dragon-bellied; grave-jawed, because grass
Is a beard that's soon shaved, and grows seldom again
    Before it is summer; so cow all the rest;
    The new Dodo is finished. O! come to my nest.

Isbrand's song is parody, parody of a cosmology of a scientific generation that will commit any sin in the name of science. Autobiography apart, we can see parody, self-parody, in the Isbrand who sings this ballad and in him who later, on the eve of his own destruction, declares: "I have a bit of FIAT in my soul." One cay play with ideas of evolution or metempsychosis if one chooses; certainly the Pythagorean theory was known to Beddoes. But it is the tone of mockery and excess that makes the poem wholly remarkable, unique in English verse; poetry as play, serious and grim play but play none the less. One dares not label as nonsense a poem that explores with humor and learning the notion of man's free will, however idiosyncratically expressed. With his Mandrake, Beddoes might have said, "Thou knowest I hunger after wisdom as the Red Sea after ghosts," and it is not strange that of the marks he chose one of the most effective should be that of the alchemistic fool: "soul of a pickle-herring, body of a spagirical toss-pot, doublet of motley, and mantle of pilgrim." All of these

personae were Beddoes, who had his bit of FIAT and died
of it. If at times he doubted himself and his gifts, he never
doubted that one of the proper functions of art is to show
men their own folly, smallness, and mortality: "O world,
world! The gods and fairies left thee for thou were too wise;
and now, thou Socratic star, thy demon, the great Pan,
Folly, is parting from thee." It is the logical paradox in
Beddoes that his science should retain strong traces of
alchemy, his poetry retain a firm grip on a tradition while
it went far from the beaten path, his morality return to a
kind of doctrine of humors while his own nature developed
most involutely.

Isbrand says of his "noble hymn to the belly gods,"
that " 'tis perhaps a little / Too sweet and tender, but that
is the fashion; / Besides my failing is too much sentiment,"
but we must not consider this irony or mere sarcasm; it is
one plane of the mask, this time a composite mask made up
of every quality Beddoes found in the poet: fool, sage, demon, beast, and monster. What does his song show us if
not the varied aspect of man's nature when he is most self-
aware and creative? The "bodiless childfull of life" exerts
will, a "bit of FIAT," and selects at last no known form of
life as its persona but the fabulous shape of the "new Dodo,"
a monstrous form of its own birthing, for the child owes no
tie to the parent that aborted it. Beddoes's abortion is an
"unborn ghost" inhabiting a limbo closer to the real world
than we suspect; if it is to come to life it will do so through
its own will and in no ordinary guise, for "the world's man-
crammed; we want no more of them." The romantic agony
of "anywhere, anywhere out of the world" was to Beddoes
a real possibility, achieveable through wisdom—science and
art. These, energized by the will, could find the single secret
of man's nature and force it to confess itself. That which
much of *Death's Jest-Book* states with seriousness and full
conviction, Isbrand's song parodies—not for the sake of
burlesque, but as another aspect of the face of life, of man:
the fool, the poet, the monstrous abortion who wills and

selects his own mask: "I'll be a new bird with the head of an ass." Man has such a head whether he knows it or not; "thou great-eared mind," Isbrand calls Mandrake. "The world will see its ears in a glass no longer," Mandrake laments now that he, the fool, is departing. "Every man is his own fool," and in his song Isbrand tells how to make the fool as unlike his usual self as possible, though however altered he may be, he will have "the head of an ass."

We can consider this song as characteristic of Beddoes in his best vain of parody: excess, conceit, and surrealism. Here is the very "fool sublimate," the formal arrangement of disgust with human life that never makes the mistake of becoming pettish. Man has no place in the world of this song, nor will Beddoes allow his "new Dodo" any of man's features save his feet—two out of six, on equal ground with a pig's and a hen's. For the rest of the creature's anatomy Beddoes raids a representative stock of lore, finding actual and fabled beasts, a whole bestiary of humors and passions. "In this dear planet of wool and of leather" he finds monsters and beasts better equipped than man to withstand the rigors of climate, and a barnyard duck has a pleasanter sound than the nightingale, the foolish bird that "sits up all midnight without any ale, / Making a noise with his nose." All normal and man-made standards shall be thrown down, all laws abandoned, all nature refashioned to suit the individual will. This has as much of the ethical as the artistic and intellectual; if not precisely "dérèglement de tous les sens," something rather closer to a genuine rebirth of the spirit through willful metamorphosis. Beddoes was far too serious as poet and scientist to write these verses with action in mind; this is the area of the grotesque, that portion of the poetic map where actuality and imagination meet in a balance so perfect that each mocks the other. We mistake the purpose of the grotesque if we look in it for what is morbid or ironic or merely fanciful; instead, it is a kind of vision which takes nothing seriously except itself, which comes from anger rather than sympathy, and which requires a lively sense of ugliness. To these ends nothing serves so well as a close association of the homely and the exotic, the exotic made homely and the homely alien. Hence, the "unborn ghost," while debating the appropriateness of becoming "an Egyptian crocodile," turns that formidable beast into a harmless absurdity, though the real nature is below this surface still. Again, addressing "serpent Lucifer," the child talks of demon and reptile as if each were innocuous, though we realize that such natures are to be considered preferable to the human. In the final stanza, Beddoes gives his sardonic contempt free rein; all beasts, all monstrous forms, real and fabled, are to join in the forming of the "new Dodo," and that portion of the "unborn ghost" not yet made flesh shall be cow: "So cow all the rest; / The new Dodo is finished. O! come to my nest." Contempt and anger, finely controlled, temper the tone, and the poem rises to a conclusion in which mingle colloquial gusto and a sinister *invitation au voyage.* As the song progresses, the rhythms become more marked, more solemn, belying the apparent lightness of statement; pauses are heavy and a broken line begins again after the caesura to rush through another line and a half, where suddenly the movement checks violently. With abrupt decision the creature completes its form and issues its sardonic invitation.

The world the creature asks us to enter is one of familiar shapes in strange combinations and positions. Entrance into such a world tests our acumen, for certain kinds of good poetry are so close to bad that the reader needs skill and taste in order to discriminate. Some kinds of bad work are more satisfying than some kinds of good, and the vices of a particular way of writing usually form the conditions of that writing's existence; that is, without the vices, there could be no writing of that sort at all. Beddoes had to be very derivative, bombastic, and coy in much of his poetry before he could suddenly generate sufficient heat to charge his power. Yet after Beddoes has made proper obeisance to the formal love story, he can suddenly surcharge banality with poetry, as in the scene between Sibylla and the ghost of her murdered lover, Wolfram:

> WOLFRAM: . . . Dar'st die?
> A grave-deep question. Answer it religiously.
> SIBYLLA: . . . With him I loved, I dared.
> WOLFRAM: . . . With me and for me.
> I am a ghost. Tremble not; fear not me.
> The dead are ever good and innocent,
> And love the living. They are cheerful creatures,
> And quiet as the sunbeams, and most like,
> In grace and patient love and spotless beauty,
> The new-born of mankind.

Similarly, in the more bloodcurdling passages, one must keep a sharp lookout lest one mistake some fine poetry for fustian; they are both there:

> ATHULF: Great and voluptuous Sin now seize upon me,
> Thou paramour of Hell's fire-crowned king,
> That showedst the tremulous fairness of thy bosom
> In heaven, and so didst ravish the best angels.

Surely bad enough. Yet Isbrand, a few lines later, tells Athulf:

> . . . Sire and mother
> And sister I had never, and so feel not
> Why sin 'gainst them should count so doubly wicked
> This side o' th' sun. If you would wound your foe,
> Get swords that pierce the mind: a bodily slice
> is cured by surgeon's butter.

If death is to a large extent the theme and subject of the play, Isbrand is death's jester, the fool of death who would turn the tables on his master only to become the more fool for his pains. At the last, Wolfram replaces on Isbrand's head the fool's cap; Sibylla's grave is decked with lilies of the valley, the plant that "bears bells":

> For even the plants, it seems, must have their fool,
> So universal is the spirit of folly;

> And whisper, to the nettles of her grave,
> "King Death hath asses' ears."

Isbrand in a sense becomes so closely identified with Death that it is with something of a shock that we finally discover him to be mortal—no supernatural creature, despite his "bit of FIAT," but a man and hence a fool. Early in the play he had tried to urge his laggard brother to join him in vengeance on the Duke; that was his greatest piece of folly, "for when he [his father's ghost] visits me in the night, screaming revenge, my heart forgets that my head wears a fool's cap." If, as Mandrake says, "all days are foaled of one mother," no man can hope to escape his lot: then indeed Isbrand and Mandrake can never be other than they are: the jesters of the world. And in the final issue, of course, men who had been fools of life are finally capped in death, becoming jesters, mocking the living and mocked at by King Death, who wears asses' ears himself. "Human kind cannot bear very much reality," Beddoes would agree, and further shows that the result of man's overreaching himself can never be other than fatal:

> ISBRAND: . . . What shall we add to man,
> To bring him higher? I begin to think
> That's a discovery I soon shall make.
> Thus, owing naught to books, but being read
> In the odd nature of much fish and fowl,
> And cabbages and beasts, I've raised myself,
> By this comparative philosophy,
> Above your shoulders, my sage gentlemen.
> Have patience but a little, and keep still;
> I'll find means bye and bye of flying higher.

Isbrand here forgets that he had earlier remarked to the apostate jester, Mandrake, "I mark by thy talk that thou commencest philosopher, and then thou art only a fellow servant out of livery." His own will, corrupted by power, has brought him to the point of believing he can transcend his humanity: "And man has tired of being merely human."

Much of *Death's Jest-Book* is fragmentary and suggestive. Occasionally there are prolepses of other poets, as in the passage immediately above. Or sometimes a packed parenthesis will suddenly lift the tone of a passage or take the reader, by powerful suggestion, into another dimension:

> ISBRAND: . . . Were I buried like him
> There in the very garrets of death's town,
> But six feet under earth, (that's the grave's sky)
> I'd jump up into life. . . .
> ZIBA: For soon the floral necromant brought forth
> A wheel of amber, (such may Clotho use
> When she spins lives). . . .

When he is going about his business properly, Beddoes is an economical writer in that he depends on verbs and strong verbal forms to do the heavy work: "I laid the lips of their two graves together, / And poured my brother into hers; while she, / Being the lightest, floated and ran over." This macabre intent of Isbrand, the repulsive nature of the deed, strike us with the greater force because of the connotation, here largely clustered about the verbs and arising from the image of liquor. At other moments he will give us poetic passages that are gently descriptive.

> ZIBA: . . . For the drug, 'tis good:
> There is a little hairy, green-eyed snake,
> Of voice like to the woody nightingale,
> And ever singing pitifully sweet,
> That nestles in the barry bones of death,
> And is his dearest pet and playfellow.
> The honied froth about that serpent's tongue
> Deserves not so his habitation's name
> As does this liquor. That's the liquor for him.

or, direct and to the immediate point,

> DUKE: . . . Nature's polluted,
> There's man in every secret corner of her,
> Doing damned wicked deeds.

The thought of power can change Isbrand's expression "like
sugar melting in a glass of poison." Again, "Never since
Hell laughed at the church, blood-drunken / From rack and
wheel, has there been joy so mad / As that which stings my
marrow now." Isbrand's hour of triumph "will be all eternal
heaven distilled / Down to one thick rich minute." In such
moments of the play, Beddoes does not need to conform to
the exigencies of a character he has created, since that character is general, not a personality. Beddoes has left out
of *Death's Jest-Book* much that modern readers want to
find if they are to feel at home, for the play frankly explores
other realities, taking risks of a sort we either do not approve
or can not see.

Still, the failure (and it is a failure) of *Death's Jest-
Book* derives not from the incomplete application of a technique, nor from a lack of talent, but from a spiritual malaise
which, if nothing else, we share with Beddoes. We have
a thousand writers who would worship "heroes of culture"
with whom a failing artist may identify himself. The weaknesses and the pathos of these "heroes" are known, but
many writers would prefer to be committed to the sins
rather than to the literature, to the personality rather than
the talent, for these are public, and they pay off in fame and
success. Pastiche, rather than eclecticism, determines such
lives and works; we are closer to romantic *mal du siècle*
than we like to think, for Hart Crane's alcohol-and-jazz
muse is easy of invocation, the nostalgics of Scott Fitzgerald
are less difficult to contrive and sustain than are the tor-
ments and passion of Dickens or Tennyson, for all their
"sentimentality." We somehow want genius to be less up-
setting, tidier; the American writer is so accustomed to
keeping his tongue in his cheek that he has trouble talking,
and he who risks a direct high tone finds the shortest shrift.
Yet it may be that we are ready for another kind of writing,
another way of observing. R. P. Blackmur has shown us
some of the uses of parody and has indicated how such a
tactic may point a way out of the slough in which modern

literature has foundered. We could use another route. Whether we accept the way of parody or not, we ought to like Beddoes; he was a man for our time a century too soon, and his work defines certain excesses we may commit, certain risks we can take, if we would wrench out of the bog.

The Complex World of
James Gould Cozzens

"It's hard to explain what I mean," says Francis Ellery, the young writer who is the chief character of *Ask Me Tomorrow*. "The situation is ironic, but also heroic. I don't think I can explain." What Francis doesn't think he can do, Cozzens undertakes to do for him and for the readers of most of Cozzens's novels. For if one can say with any certainty that there is *a* theme for the best of the books, it would seem to be this: the double vision of modern man, the central paradox of action and contemplation, of understanding and conduct, of the ironic view and the heroic efficacy.

That such a theme has concerned many writers of our age a short view of the literature evidences. With most novelists, however, we become aware that the attempt is to describe the split between the worlds of action and thought or to celebrate the one as opposed to the other. *The Magic Mountain* redresses the balance overset by *The Sun Also Rises*; *The Sound and the Fury* supplies the lack we feel after *A Passage to India*; suffering from *The Portrait of the Artist as a Young Man*, we later find a cure, perhaps, in Graham Greene's *The End of the Affair*. In each reaction from the previous action, we are as readers victims of polarities, willing ones to be sure, but none the less victims. It has been, I think, the peculiar contribution of Cozzens to the twentieth-century novel that what goes on in his books is a dramatization of experience within that whole gamut stretching between the poles, the region of our experience, the places in which we live and die and work. And of course there is nothing new in this, though much of it has been forgotten. Cozzens is the legitimate heir of George Eliot and, nearer to our own day, of Conrad. However pedestrian or exotic the worlds of the novels of these two writers, the question usually resolves itself thus: What do these people *do* and what strange concatenation of luck, logic, and living has brought them to this pass? Within the huge area thus described lies the central and ultimate dependence. With few expressed assumptions as to the proper conduct of life in general, Cozzens creates a world of particulars, a world of men and women at their tasks and duties, and then tries to show the intricacy of the web of will and desire, the stuff of action, as these work out in men's involvement with one another, with themselves, with their tasks—all of these relationships described with irony, shown in action, brought to a climax best characterized as heroic.

General statements of this sort are of little use without a full knowledge of the novels themselves, and I fear that Cozzens has fewer readers than he deserves, largely because there are difficulties in the way of an estimate of worth, difficulties of fashion and technique, and even more than these, difficulties of basic assumption about the nature of the world and the point of vantage from which one observes the world. Cozzens has few companions in our time, among novelists at least; among poets E. A. Robinson shares certain attributes with him. All this seems to indicate something that should be stressed by any critic of Cozzens: his entire method and technique have an appearance of old-fashioned discursiveness, of a certain formidable denseness of surface best described, again, as old-fashioned.

Not that Cozzens's novels, with the exception of *Guard of Honor*, are very long; most say what they need to say in the (formerly) canonical three hundred pages or thereabouts. Nor does Cozzens overwhelm us with realistic detail or delicately conceived and highly wrought personal insights. On the whole, the form and texture of these novels are traditional, conservative, and uncomplicated. The trouble lies just there: expecting certain kinds of formal qualities which in turn create the further expectancy of finding certain sorts of meaning, we are deterred at the very start by a sensibility which, being tough, demands toughness. We can fit Cozzens nowhere into the survey course.

He sees through our feelings, and we do not like it. For like most of the characters in most of the novels, we cling to what we know, fearing the loss of identity that comes with the double vision. Like Francis Ellery, cursed with a sense of complexity, we would go just so far and then turn back when the going gets tough; perhaps unlike Francis, most of us make the turn with—well, if not success, at least ease.

Initiation into the world of complexity, not mere complication, is then one aspect of Cozzens's scheme, and for most of his heroes there is the constant struggle with fact and with self. Many of the protagonists are men of mature age—Ross in *Guard of Honor*, Dr. Bull in *The Last Adam*, Ernest Cudlipp in *Men and Brethren*—and these characters in their various ways have worked out for themselves a mode of action and a standard of conduct by which they judge others and by which we as readers may judge them. They have passed the age when character may be said to be forming still; it is now a question of what is to be done with the life thus set, and of course Cozzens sees that life as one of profession, work, and of the vision a man has of himself and the work he does. Colonel Ross, with his trained legal mind and his trained use of the double vision, can play his Chiron to General Beal's Achilles—the ironist to the hero— and can in the course of three days make a mature man out of a hot pilot. He can work this miracle because all things work together for complexity for those able to see it and do something with it. If in the gathering excitement of *Guard of Honor* the more critical of us think we must be on guard against the meretricious, against a *Caine Mutiny*, we would do well to think here of Conrad in *Nostromo*. If on the other hand we look in Cozzens's novels for kinds of techniques and styles we tend to associate with significant writing, we should remember, for example, Milton: the fact that a writer does not write a certain way does not mean he cannot. The Faulknerian purple patch or the rhapsodies of *nada* and sleeping bag may not be beyond a writer's powers; they may be simply outside his purposes.

The gross stimulant of the idiosyncratic has a proper function in art, but that function is ephemeral. George Borrow and Ronald Firbank do not necessarily cure what ails us any better than Henry James and George Bernard Shaw. Often what captures us in a writer is the sense of power in reserve, of potency. We know that Milton could and did write a "Comus" and do not therefore say that a further exploration of the vein was beyond his powers. We can read *Paradise Lost* or *Samson Agonistes* and consider a few masques well forgone for this gift.

Power in potency as well as in efficacy—this Cozzens preeminently has. Here is God's plenty, in range of action and feeling, in virile prose style, in setting, in character, in humor. Do you like novels of great scope and variety? Try *Guard of Honor*. Do you like the packed, delicate analytic work of insight into character and moral decision? *Ask Me Tomorrow* should satisfy. Do you prefer a realistic treatment of ordinary folk going about their lives and ways, yet with a heightened awareness? *The Just and the Unjust* should answer. In all these books Cozzens dramatizes significant action while he gives a sense of power in reserve and varies pace and tone so adeptly as to convey a sense of mastery, of mature, unself-conscious command of the medium almost unique in American fiction. The irony does not destroy the heroism, nor does the heroic purpose annihilate the complexity.

Such achievement is, as Cozzens observes through the sensibility of Miro in *S.S. San Pedro*, "a matter of *tela*, of form." That fatal word, *form*. I believe that preeminently among contemporary writers Cozzens has rediscovered aspects of form, of the formal observances that constitute the good manners of fiction, which most of us have not found lately and have therefore stopped looking for; the sense for them has begun to atrophy. And since the appetite for art is artificial, cultivated, art itself can lose attributes that make it the more artful while we search for glossier trim. The gross stimulant of rhetoric, in lieu of style, makes us perhaps insensitive to real prose, the kind of prose that avoids excesses and ranges back and forth between the poles of bare simplicity and a highly wrought complexity—never, though, resting at the poles themselves. Such a style Cozzens commands: avoidance of extremes without either insipidity or dullness; it is only thus that a novelist can keep his style supple, useful for many purposes. It is, I believe, the triumph of the fine novelist that he be able to suggest boredom without boring, dullness without dulling, tumidity without flatulence. It is "a matter of *tela*, of form." Things are "going as they should go—tight, smart." And above all, someone is doing a job of work, for a purpose, for delight, for wisdom, in many tones of voice and between the hysterical poles where lies the country of universal human experience. It is a multivocal tone. If one wants strict point of view, *Ask Me Tomorrow* will provide that, but in a sense the problem of form in these novels is denser than a consideration of what tricks can be played. We can look at it this way: among contemporary novelists Cozzens is unique in the use of a ratiocinative technique superimposed on a dramatic, almost melodramatic, subject matter, and one of the excitements of the best work derives from the tension vibrating between these seeming irreconcilabilities. For example, in *Guard of Honor* the first section of the novel moves back and forth in time while the actual chronological duration of the focal situation consumes some four hours; we meet many of the important characters; the heroic exploits of Bus Beal are thrillingly recounted, spiced with the appropriate ironic comment in the mind of Ross, the ratiocinative observer whose sensibility and speculative intelligence control the tone and meaning; and the section ends with the near-catastrophe at the landing field, the slugging of the Negro pilot, and the breaking of a violent thunderstorm. Throughout, we are aware of where we are—in an airplane over inland Florida. Cozzens creates with care and economy the spare, functional setting and the general ambience compounded of technical detail, rumor of war, and the relativity of time.

The atmosphere thus set persists throughout the book. One of the ironies in this heroic narrative derives from the juxtaposition of the petty and the vast, a motif that expresses itself in opposition of character, of incident, and of mood. All the people in this book do things. There is a war on, and they have duties to perform, often in conflict with their desires and best gifts, but war and life exact their services. The better adjusted folk, the men of single vision, act their parts ritualistically, formally, like the master and technical sergeants of the Knock and Wait Club, whereas the complex, or potentially complex, characters must do and act in a welter of indecision, mixed motives, and self-scrutiny, like Ross and Hicks. It is one of the great affirmations of Cozzens's work that he knows his men of double vision for doers as well as seers—doers of evil at times, perhaps, but never mere self-pitying impotents letting I-dare-not wait upon I-would. They are men, living and trying to clean up the messes left by the grown-up adolescents with whom their lot is of necessity cast. As Ross observes, the guard of honor should be for the living, not for the dead. The empty ceremonies in which we engage in order to make palatable or attractive those tasks that would otherwise appall cannot satisfy men cursed with the double vision, those who, tragically perhaps and certainly ironically, must be the doers the very while that they see most clearly the magnitude of the work and the inadequacy of the tools, their own and everyone else's. Hence much of the overt irony revolves about the eternal point of the discrepancy between the way things look and the way they are, between reality as it must be taken if we are to live fully in it and reality as men so often corrupt it to make their delusions viable. And that Cozzens may the more dramatically vivify his multifarious theme, he peoples his story with characters whose relation to the theme is expressed by each one's degree of maturity, his awareness of things as they really are. Captain Andrews is a mathematical genius and a person of sweetness and simplicity, and his view of the world and of the nature of life is preposterous. General Nichols, that "stripped-down, comfortless, plain and simple mind," may from the rarified height of his aloofness see the others as "superannuated children," may see that "each childish adult determinedly bet his life and staked his sacred pride on, say, the Marxist's ludicrous substance of things only hoped for, or the Christian casuist's wishful evidence of things not so much as seen." Yet his is the simpler nature. In the end, the hot flyboy Bus Beal, who has come to the realization of complexity, has the last word, over Nichols and all the rest:

> "Jo-Jo [Nichols] thinks I need a nurse. That's you. I guess I do act that way." He laughed. "Don't worry, Judge," he said. He put his hand suddenly on Colonel Ross's shoulder. "Even Jo-Jo knows they could do without him before they could do without me. That's not boasting, Judge. There's a war on. Jo-Jo can talk to Mr. Churchill; but the war, that's for us. Without me—without us, he wouldn't have a whole hell of a lot to talk about, would he?"

He includes Ross with himself and himself with Ross. Attaining to the double vision without consequent loss of power means maturity for Beal, and responsibility. From now on, when he will act as he must, he must also say, with Ross, "I really saw nobody all day who was not in one way or another odious. . . . And of course in every situation I was odious, too." Whether or not Mrs. Beal can emulate Mrs. Ross and say, " 'I know.' . . . She moved until her head rested against his shoulder. 'Let's not go on about it,' " is perhaps uncertain. What the reader knows is that the guard of honor should indeed be for the living.

This novel is certainly Cozzens's most detailed, most complex dramatization of the complex theme; yet most of the others, each in its own particular way, show the unending struggle of the main characters for unity within diversity, for a tough sense of the actual coupled with a love for life and people. One of the basic lessons Francis Ellery, in *Ask Me Tomorrow*, must learn, in suffering and near-despair, is the lesson of human limitation, that you cannot eat your cake and have it too. Abner Coates, in *The Just and the Unjust*, goes to the same hard school. Cozzens does not pretend that school is fun and "learning—experiences"; it is, plainly, life, and though he does not minimize the pain and the humiliation, neither does he romanticize suffering nor celebrate solemnity. Cozzens's heroes are serious, not solemn, and they have humor or at least find humor and pleasure in their routines, their loves, their daily work. Living can be, for them, all of a piece because while their vision of the world is multiform, the incapacitating effect of such vision is forestalled by their delight in living and working—in their curiosity about people, their delight in the exercise of their own powers, in their fine sense of the rich surprise and humor of life. It amounts to love, love with a sense "of *tela*, of form."

Nowhere does this dense feeling for life emerge more clearly than in the style. I know of no modern novelist who commands such a range of idiom, allusion, cadence, rhetorical radiation, and vocabulary. It is a muscular, virile style with certain strong affinities to seventeenth-century prose; Cozzens is fond of Bunyan, Milton, and Defoe, among others. Yet one does not get the feeling of reading a "literary" novel. The ironic view alone prevents this. For the ordinary reader the allusiveness and learning serve two purposes: they give a sense of mind in operation and they remind him that the intellectual faculties are here taken seriously, as a vital part of living. Moreover, the method of Cozzens in this regard is to make both the learned allusion and its application appropriate to his character. Abner Coates does not show a great range of knowledge and erudition, though his father does, and properly so. Ernest Cudlipp, an Anglican priest, should and does have views on and, ideally at least, considerable scholarly knowledge of, Barthian theology, the Thirty-nine Articles, and the music of Bach. And it is not at all surprising that Colonel Ross, trained in the old school, should have by heart lines from *Samson Agonistes*. Cozzens does not, then, wish to impress us with his learning. What does impress us, however, is the flexibility of the style and the mastery of tone which allow a writer to shift from the highly idiomatic speech of contemporary characters to allusive play while at the same time no violent wrenching, no destruction of tone, spoils matters for mind and ear alike. One could quote many characteristic passages, or present the magnificently comic yet pathetic scene of Francis Ellery's entrapment by Mr. McKellar, the learned amateur of all the arts, the incredible windbag. It is a devastating portrait and a scene dramatic with many shifts and shades, tonal and ironic. And throughout the style operates, not for and by itself, but accommodating itself to the situation and its tone, to the speaker, to the ones spoken to, and above all to the totality of the theme to be dramatized. I can do no better here than to give three sentences describing, through Francis's sensibility, Mr. McKellar's discourse:

> With paeans and apostrophes he contrasted the state of creatures living as nature meant them to, and of man, living as a foul and flagitious civilization dictated. Spoken by Mr. McKellar, the English language died in extremity, was solemnly buried, and rose again having put on incorruption. It became more English, not in the imitative sense of resembling an Englishman's speech—until Mr. McKellar took up his residence there such an accent could hardly ever have been heard in England—but absolutely, in the sense of resembling a Platonic ideal, with "a's" so extraordinary that the most supercilious don would have to go down, and Mr. McKellar bore the palm alone.

It is high humor, and the diction (who since Pope has dared use that adjective *flagitious*, even if he knew what it meant?) and the syntax take much of the credit for the effect. Cozzens's vocabulary is huge, its use precise, its tonal range satisfyingly various. He does not depend on the unusual word, the shock of lack of recognition. A passage of this sort, from *Guard of Honor*, shows what he can do with the simplest elements:

> Moderately warmed by whiskey, Nathaniel Hicks took a look at the blonde girl on what might be called his own account; yet where Captain Wiley saw such a temptingly available delicacy, all Nathaniel Hicks saw was a lot of trouble. Reason, indeed, overcomes the passions! If, by lifting his finger now, he could enjoy her, would he lift it? He would not! He would go further than that. If—an improbable hypothesis, since he was not exactly Captain Wiley—the propositioning was hers; if she provided, with no work of finger-lifting, the necessary time and place to "organize" her: if she then and there offered herself to him, free of bother and uncertainty of going after her, would he accept? He felt safe in saying he would, instead, get the hell out the shortest way.

The possibilities for humor and contrast in such a stylistic tone are apparent; the general toughness of syntax, that masculine power which, though not drawing attention to itself is always there and shows itself on analysis, informs the best of all Cozzens's work. Whether one selects such a passage as that from *S.S. San Pedro* describing a vessel turning over her main engines at the pier, or something like the last paragraph of Section I of *Guard of Honor*, the enduring impression remains one of power, hard intellectuality, and humanity.

Style cannot divorce content satisfactorily; they stay married happily or unhappily. Cozzens has always chosen difficult subjects for his novels, and if it can be said that both vocabulary and syntax reflect and vivify the toughness of his thought, it can equally be declared that the increasing complexity of the worlds he chooses for the milieux of his novels augments the power of his theme. If one goes back to the quotation from *Ask Me Tomorrow*, one can see per-

haps only a happy wit and a precise economy of style; in
context, however, the passage has many overtones, for
there we find another aspect of the theme of expatriate
Americans, another ironic juxtaposition, another accentu-
ation of the pathos of Francis's position, a further range of
complexity in the allusion to a type. Mr. McKellar is—who?
Ford Madox Ford? It scarcely matters, for we know *him*,
whoever he may be.

What we continue increasingly to discover in these
novels as they grow in maturity and depth is the constant
theme of the heroic, and perhaps its converse, the craven;
in *Castaway*, near-allegory; in *S.S. San Pedro*, a suggestion
of symbolism, and a dramatization of the heroic, cheek by
jowl with the ordinary, the craven, the simply dutiful. Yet
after all, in the presentation of life as it strikes the sensibility and intellect of the novelist, what must occur if not
the vision of reality and man's unceasing, seemingly unsuccessful attempt to cope with it? Reality viewed as the
intractable given, about which nothing can be done and
which we ignore at our peril—no highflown peril to some
impossibly delicate putative antennae, but to a man's liveli-
hood, body, and immortal soul. And Cozzens's heroes fight
for life, the life that old Judge Coates speaks for at the end
of *The Just and the Unjust*, or which Ernest Cudlipp in
Men and Brethren sees all about him, in a prurient elevator
boy, an unfaithful wife, a shattered Alaskan missionary,
a homosexual renegade monk. Life is everywhere, and not
good just because it is life, but always heroic when most it
fulfills its true nature and makes for more and fuller life.
And life has much meaning here: growth, maturity, wisdom, loving kindness, variousness, honor. Never abstract,
these qualities come before us in the novels; we see the
hero smug in his security gradually being stripped to—
well, perhaps a General Nichols, but far better in the long
run to a Francis Ellery or a Colonel Ross. Even as they go
through their *peine forte et dure*, these latter come to accept and embrace the world. It is, finally, love; love with

belief, and with belief both responsibility and the wisdom deriving therefrom.

Wisdom may be the answer for Cozzens and his heroes; neither Achilles nor Hector, but Odysseus. In so far as a man lacks the capacity to enter into another's nature and understand it, at least partially, he lacks heroic stature; in so far as the man of vision is paralyzed by the baffling dimensions of that vision, he is the mere ironist: "How I despise such mere men of Muscle!" Dr. Bull, in *The Last Adam*, is ultimately unsatisfying as a protagonist, as a hero, for his very lack of vision, as Mr. Banning in the same novel fails to satisfy as a foil to Bull because he lacks muscle to pursue his vision and make it workable in his life. He retreats into his money and his taste. Yet why not, really? That is the way things go in life. In the later novels, Cozzens does, I think, take a long stride ahead. Not content simply to show things as he sees them in their essence to be—in all their vital complexity of technique and demand for mastery or botch—he develops a suppler style and a more profound insight into the nature of vitality in its fullest sense. The worlds of the later novels—*Men and Brethren. The Just and the Unjust, Ask Me Tomorrow, Guard of Honor*—grow more complex, in step with the increasing richness of the minds of the characters, while the range of allusion and application broadens, and the technical detail becomes thicker, the life described denser. This capacity for growth has always been unusual in American writers. Yet Cozzens has for one reason or another remained out of fashion and the public (or critical) eye may have contributed to this growth, and few will summon the dubious charity to wish him a sudden vogue.

Yet the question of a lack of serious attention to Cozzens's work cannot be set aside simply because one knows full well the damage done to American writers by an undeserved or disproportionate popularity; clearly the opposite danger has in our century done an equal amount of harm. If in this discussion of Cozzens's novels I have placed large emphasis on the intellectual elements in his work, I do not wish to imply that the novels are mere *contes philosophiques* or theses; I reiterate, if the method seems at times to be ratiocinative, speculative, analytic, the matter thus explored is none the less dramatic. From the beginning (ignoring those first ventures that Cozzens himself would surely wish to expunge) the wedding of his spiritual, physical, and moral crises has been his concern, and, of course, the desideratum of the more thoughtful critics of our time. What else have we asked for all these years in our art? Why do the book-reviewers continually call for some new Tolstoy who will bring together sweeping action and genuine theme? Why have we tired of those so terribly perceptive insight-vendors, by Henry James out of Ford Madox Ford? As Edmund Wilson pointed out not so very long ago, Franz Kafka is not necessarily good for what ails us, nor should we complain when Herman Wouk sweeps all before him; what else are we offered? In poetry we have fared better; the vitality we long to find has caught us up in the work of Yeats, Auden, the later Eliot. If we look to the novel for art as well as crudeness, sometimes confused with power, we are hard put to it to name anyone. We lament this state of affairs; the voices of J. Donald Adams and R. P. Blackmur are raised simultaneously if cacophonously, and everyone wants power, wisdom, moral vision. How else explain the Conrad revival? The rediscovery of Dickens and George Eliot? The awed admiration for *The Adventures of Augie March*? Casting about for some signs that the novel did not die while we dozed over *The Disguises of Love* and *The Groves of Academe*, we seize on any *big* (thick) book and after we have assured ourselves that it could not possibly suit Hollywood, we take comfort in the continued existence of the old bourgeois epic. And all the time, quietly and with attention neither from Hollywood nor the literary quarterlies, James Gould Cozzens has written at least three novels, perhaps four, to rank with the best of our time. Does this sound familiar? Did anything of this sort happen before? Hawthorne? Melville? Dickinson? Robinson? It has happened before, and to the best of our artists. Why should it seem particular with them?

Fashion of course plays a major part, yet when one has said that, one needs to discover what elements in the prevailing or succeeding fashions have militated against the suitable reception of a fine novelist. Certainly Cozzens is far too complex and tough an author to appeal to a wide audience—in his own time, at any rate. As for the smaller audience—the one that reads Dylan Thomas, T. S. Eliot, and Robert Frost, the one that is eager to find out about good reading when it can be assured it is *good*—the smallest audience has not yet passed down the word on Cozzens. The smallest audience (critics, writers, even some professors) does not want to bother, having settled for Faulkner and Hemingway, and that should be enough for one generation. After all, Hemingway is set—the first and the last are the one book, and in his beginning is his end. We know all about it, or think we do. Myth. Ritual. Nada. Cojones. As for Faulkner, he is dead and gone and safely in the DAB. I have no intention of flinging mud at writers who cannot be smirched by such a foolish gesture; I would remark merely that we have overlooked a whole tradition, and the occasional attempts to recapture it have failed because we looked in the wrong places. The intense discipline of the craft of fiction that James and Conrad taught us to revere, and which we delight to throw over when we switch to Dreiser, has somehow led us to believe that high art cannot be dissociated from preciosity, from sensibility perplexed in the extreme. Only lately have we come to the Conrad of *Nostromo*; it should not be much of a step to *Guard of Honor*. The chief difficulty lies in Cozzens's uncompromising refusal to mix genres and to simplify theme. He insists on writing prose and on pursuing the uneasy question of the lives *we live*; we can like it or lump it. This is not to say that no one has ever lived in the fashion of Studs Lonigan or of Milly Theale; it is simply that most of us rather take that on faith. In the case of Cozzens's novels we could use a little less faith and more simple understanding. His characters belong to trades and professions and towns and milieux the way Dickens's folk belong to some special way of living. If for the modern reader there is something of the exotic in a Chadband or a Wemmick, there need not necessarily have been such an appeal when *Bleak House* and *Great Expectations* first appeared. The exotic elements for the modern reader are none the less compelling; and in Cozzens's novels the world of types explored by Dickens and by Shaw and by Ben Jonson comes before us again in its unfamiliar shape—the shape of the local, urban, and workaday, qualities too trivial to most novelists in recent years to seem worthy of their attention. Cozzens forces our attention, concentrates it, makes us inescapably aware of the density of the lives we lead.

The double vision, the awareness of complexity, affects not only style and character but, most important of all, action. I have mentioned the near-melodramatic tinge sometimes assumed by Cozzens's plots, but this tells us no more than that the books deal in incident piled on incident, in violence at times, and in large scenes of catastrophe: shipwreck and near-panic in *S.S. San Pedro*, a trial for murder in *The Just and the Unjust*, terror and the killing of a lunatic in *Castaway*, various episodes of death and near-death in *Guard of Honor*. In thus packing his novel with action, Cozzens again seems to be reverting to an old-fashioned conception of the milieu, to a conception with epic qualities. The purpose has more to do with the novelistic than the sociological; that is, I do not believe Cozzens is trying to tell us that modern life is violent and that modern novels should therefore show violence, though there may be much truth in such a contention. Nor is the purpose merely the exposition of the theme of good and evil. I think the answer lies, as I hope I have suggested, in a view at once simpler and more profound. He takes, a priori, the position that life is a tragic affair. The novel does not illustrate the view; rather, the action, in the Aristotelian sense, departs from this initial point, leaving it always there, as the given, the transparent window through which we view the unfolding action in its perspectives. Though this departure has elements of originality, Cozzens can nevertheless be reckoned the legitimate heir of Hawthorne and Melville, and perhaps of Poe. Unmistakably American in his peculiar moral vision, he refines on the rationale of many American writers by taking as the very base and fabric of that vision, and the cosmology it would observe, a sternly Calvinistic (with qualifications) measure of grace, salvation, and works. Whether his knowledge of seventeenth-century writers contributes to this attitude I cannot say; in any event, the Melville of *Billy Budd* and the Hawthorne of "Young Goodman Brown" would find no difficulty with these novels. And I am sure that Poe would envy Cozzens's *Castaway* and much of *Guard of Honor*. Moral obliquity, the question of salvation by grace or by works, or by neither, the problem of power and its necessity—these are central issues in the work of our best writers, and Cozzens takes them as given. Within the mode of the realistic novel he contrives a single action to which all characters and incidents relate. As we see the complexities arise we involve ourselves in the world of these characters, but we do not at any point empathize to a degree destructive of the basic assumption; to the point at which we are able to say comfortingly to ourselves, "Everything is relative." Cozzens forces us to look unflinchingly at the relativity of all things, at degrees of justice and injustice, for example, and Abner Coates, the young attorney, works out his destiny between the poles of total rejection of responsibility and assumption of a cynical relativism. He is neither Goodman Brown nor Captain Delano. It may be that his father is a sort of Captain Vere. For most of Cozzens's characters of heroic stature, the nature of the Shavian "master of reality" becomes the object of their struggle. The novels move outward with the quest for reality, vision, and direction.

The descriptive term *old-fashioned* comes to a very great deal more, ultimately, than the matter of techniques. The traditional view of American writers, much discussed in our own time but rarely dramatized in literature, takes shape in Cozzens's novels. Of course, it is idle to force the point and play games of reducing all American novels to two types, the Huck and the Ahab, pleasant occupation though it may be. For one thing, Cozzens is far more at home in his world of fact and technique than ever Melville and Hawthorne could be; the temptation toward allegory that they could never resist, Cozzens transmutes in his best work into an urge for complex vision. He has found in a man's work and his means of objectifying his desires the mythos or world view comfortable and appropriate to his gift. That he has grown and matured in power and profundity seems proof of this; from May Tupping of *The Last Adam* to Ross of *Guard of Honor*, his masters of reality deepen in understanding and compassion while their view of the world multiplies its vistas to conform to the increased size of the stage they must occupy and try to dominate. None of these characters loses awareness of self for all the awareness of the dangers of self-pity. Humor remains at the worst of times; however catastrophic the event may prove, there is always the trying and the illimitable curiosity; understanding and belief will come from the trying, given luck and as much good management as a man is capable of. As Judge Coates says at the very end of *The Just and the Unjust*, "We just want you to do the impossible." To the tragic, the ironic-and-heroic sensibility, simple answers are an impossibility because they derive from wrong questions. Life consists of messes; it is the job of some to make them, that of others to clean them up; an impossible task, and we do it every day. That task underlies the action of Cozzens's novels. Yet cleaning up or messing up is what the characters do and becomes the measure of the men: masters of reality, slaves of delusion, casualties of fact. To the mind imbued with a New England sense of the tragic, to a Hawthorne or a Robinson or a Cozzens, what counts is the stubbornest fact of all: life and death, and the two are one. Ironic, perhaps. Acceptance and the struggle to achieve it confer the heroic wisdom.

What Edith Wharton Saw in Innocence

It seems unlikely that in putting down my feelings about *The Age of Innocence* I will entirely escape the charge—always justified—of prejudice. One tends in criticism to use a work or a writer as a stick with which to beat other works and writers, or worse still, other critics, with the result that the book one is concerned with rather escapes. This danger looms larger in the case of the best-known novels and poems, those works which have created schools, reputations, endowed chairs and new stacks in libraries. I have no such oppressive imminence above me in this instance. We all await the release, some fourteen years hence, of Edith Wharton's private papers, and although most students of American literature know the Wharton name and may have read *Ethan Frome*, too few seem to have become acquainted with the entire reach of her work, much of which, one has to confess at once, has value only for the specialist. *The Age of Innocence* has been variously judged, and one of the more recent critics of Edith Wharton places it rather lower than *The House of Mirth*, a judgment with which I disagree, largely, in this instance, because I think the critic seriously misreads the novel.

But all such matters apart, one still has the problem of telling readers, some in the know, some outside, just what it is that strikes oneself as distinctive and impressive about the book. How to get the reader to go back to *The Age of Innocence* convinced of pleasure and profit to come? Times and readers change, but this novel, written at the height of Edith Wharton's powers, retains a power the gradual release of which one becomes aware of with time, with acquaintance, with a more delicate attuning of the ear and the sensibility to the things Edith Wharton was writing about. And it seems to me one of the graces and delights of *The*

Age of Innocence lies exactly in the multifariousness of its thematic material, in its refusal to tie itself down to "meaning," the while that it glitters with a density, a hardness of surface that only a truly novelistic eye could have seen and an informing mind recreate.

The seeing is the thing. What does Conrad say? "It is above all to make you *see* . . . and it is everything." I know of no other American novelist with Edith Wharton's power (in this book, at any rate) of simple vision, of showing us who was there and in what grouping, what juxtapositions. The very opening moment of the novel, the scene at the opera, serves as an example: Newland Archer and his beautifully dressed, languidly self-assured companions, the tenor and the soprano on the ornate stage, May Welland all in white and pink. Then comes the entrance into the Mingott box of the Countess Olenska, the dark lady of this plot! Nowhere does Edith Wharton's grip relax; her hold on actuality is everywhere firm. She has been there—she knows. From the smallest flower in the Beaufort conservatory to the styling of dresses by Worth in the 1870s—she knows it all and she knows how to put it before us in all its appeal of the rare, the far-off, the perhaps absurd. And in so doing, she does not patronize either her readers or her characters and their world; in fact, the irony cuts several ways at once, with the result that those of us who succumb to the temptation of contempt for fashionable New York society in the 1870s get our comeuppance. She does not flatter us with the delusion that we have progressed or found a new freedom. We have simply changed masters.

The scenes that strike us so vividly throughout the novel are of different sorts, and not one seems there for its own sake. The wonderfully vivid tableau of May, the still-glowing, Dianaesque matron on the lawn at Newport, bow at shoulder, while the rosy girls watch her marksmanship and the idle gentlemen assess the ladies and their quality—there is surely no delight in mere grouping and bric-a-brac, though such delight is legitimate on the author's part and ours, but a lively sense of surface and attitude, without which no deeper probing is possible. And the probing takes us deep enough for comfort, down to the quick of a society, a world, a whole history of the American sensibility.

That indeed seems to emerge as the finest quality of Edith Wharton's theme in *The Age of Innocence*, the whole question of the old and the new, of passion and duty, of the life of the feelings and that of the senses. For us, reading the book some thirty-five years after its publication, the complexities of meaning alone make the novel seem far richer than many another more highly touted. And again, here is no apparatus composed of symbols, near-allegory, and didacticism, but a tissue of objects, places, attitudes, and desires.

If one can plump for a single "meaning" that the book may hold for us today, it may well be that of the lost life of feeling, the kind of life, the kinds of feeling, that Newland Archer's son seems utterly incapable of understanding or knowing. At the very end, when Newland Archer, for the last time, retreats from Ellen Olenska and from the sort of experience his son Dallas is only too glad to meet, we feel the fullness of the irony. Archer, with his insecurity, his sensitivity, and his passion, has obeyed the moral imperatives of his class and time and has given up Ellen and love for the furtherance of the shallow-seeming aims, all amorphous as they are, of his world. He has stuck to May and to his New York, giving up another world.

What has he gained in return? Another writer would perhaps say, quite simply, "Nothing" and indict the time and himself along with it, but of course to Edith Wharton "everything is true in a different sense." What Newland has lost is not Ellen, but May, whom he never took pains to know or love; May who knew all along the extent and the fullness of her husband's "sacrifice." That the first inkling

Archer gains of this should come from the casual, almost
flippant, remarks of his son Dallas adds another twist to the
ironic knot. What does Dallas know of the life of the feelings and passions, he who has always known who he is,
what he wants, where he is going? He has only to ask and
it is straightaway made clear to him: "What's the use of
making mysteries?" says Dallas, "It only makes people want
to nose 'em out." And we quite agree, knowing with our
unerring hindsight that the best that can be said for Dallas's
world is that he and his fellows knew not what mysteries
they made, whereas Archer and his contemporaries most
certainly did. For Dallas, it would have been so simple:
run away with Ellen Olenska, and hang what people will
say. It is no longer necessary for him to run and scandalize
in order that he may enjoy Fanny Beaufort. Times have
changed, and in this simpler and freer world of Dallas's
young manhood, there are no occasions to exercise the feelings nor nourish passion. Like every son who ever was, he
can see in the married life of his parents only the grim, the
incommunicable, the faintly ludicrous:

> ". . . you date, you see, dear old boy.
> But mother said . . ."
> "Your mother?"
> "Yes: the day before she died. It was when she sent
> for me alone—you remember? She said she knew we were
> safe with you and always would be, because once, when
> she asked you to, you'd given up the thing you most
> wanted."
> Archer received this communication in silence. . . . At
> length he said in a low voice: "She never asked me."
> "No. I forgot. You never did ask each other anything,
> did you? And you never told each other anything. You
> just sat and watched each other, and guessed at what was
> going on underneath. A deaf-and-dumb asylum, in fact!
> Well, I back your generation for knowing more about each
> other's private thoughts than we ever have time to find out
> about our own.—I say, Dad," Dallas broke off, "you're not

angry with me? If you are, let's make it up and go and
lunch at Henri's. I've got to rush out to Versailles afterward."

For Dallas, it is just that simple—and what a knot of irony
has tightened in this brief passage! Can Dallas or anyone
like him begin to understand the meaning of the kind of
feelings Archer has known? Have they the time? the imagination? the passion? What can the notion of a buried life
mean to one who can conceive only of surface? As Archer
himself puts it to himself, "The thing one's so certain of in
advance: can it ever make one's heart beat wildly?"

Newland Archer does not say this to his son. Times
have changed, and the steady cultivation of the affections,
of nuances of feeling which only an ordered society allows
seems to the new generation "a deaf and dumb asylum."
Dallas and his contemporaries have a kindly contempt for
such old-fashioned, illiberal notions and would throw down
all the canons by which a rigid society governs its members. Archer, who sees that "there [is] good in the new
order too" still asks:

> What was left of the little world he had grown up in,
> and whose standards had bent and bound him?

And again:

> "That's it: they [Dallas's generation] feel equal to
> things—they know their way about," he mused, thinking
> of his son as the spokesman of the new generation which
> had swept away all the old landmarks, and with them the
> sign-posts and the danger-signals.

And the danger signals! The innocence of Newland Archer,
to think that the society of which he was a part could set
and keep the life it sought—could hold it, make it last by
occasional raids on dissenters and backsliders by the van
der Luydens, come down in all their minatory splendor from
Skuytercliff—to keep offenders in line! All dreadfully
amusing; and yet . . . And yet the innocence of Dallas to

propose remaking the world and human nature, to think that to cast off one form of bondage means freedom!

Here (one hesitates on the threshold of sociology) we are back at the Americanism of our novel and the old saw of American innocence, the curious underside of it that the novelists (the best of them) alone can show us. What have we here in Newland Archer but Lambert Strether seen from another point of view, and from both points he figures as American. My lost youth. Lost, all lost. The discovery, too late, that what one had known as final is all too patently, seen from here and now, no such matter. If James would in some sort show us that America is too simple, too unknowing, Edith Wharton seems to be saying that only if America can evolve a society that feels deeply and can say what it feels can it do more than shift from generation to generation, without a sense of the past, without depth, without blessing. What to feel with and about, we wonder, contemplating the prospect. *The Age of Innocence* makes this clear enough, I think, to us who have rather more sense of what the Dallases of the twentieth century have got us into, all innocent as they were. Is there nothing admirable in the total commitment of May to her world and to Newland Archer? Nothing of the heroic? For I believe that if any character in this novel partakes of the heroic nature it is indeed May Welland, she of the pink and white surface and the candid glance, whose capacity for passion and sacrifice her husband never knew. And—irony again—her son Dallas sees it all so clearly, but it is to him "prehistoric," "dated." The innocence of May Welland, so perfectly adjusted to her society, so much a product of "race, moment, milieu," takes on at least a kind of grandeur that, if we put any stock at all these days in the uncommon, approaches the tragic.

Edith Wharton is very clear about all of this: She opposes Archer, the near-rebel, with May, the total conformist. Here a lesser novelist would have been content to rest, in the mere showing of the processes by which an American with separatist tendencies is broken to harness and curb.

That she does not leave it at this adds dimension to the book and to the novelist's vision. The emphasis here rests finally upon the ways in which an individual, in more or less settled times, can come to identify his illusions with those of his world. The rightness or wrongness of such identification we may determine if we can, though for my part I would say that the triumph of Edith Wharton's realism strikes one as most sweeping in just her very refusal to draw any such line; she seems merely to say, that is the way things were for these people. Had you done differently, it would have been a different time, place, and cast.

If this novel is not quite a retelling of *Bérénice* there is in it some, at least, of Racine's sense of fatality and of the course of duty as a form of fate to be defied at one's peril. As Archer quite clearly sees, to follow one's simple duty means that one must in some sense lose one's life. Yet this is not really the tragedy for Archer; it comes at last, as we have seen, to his final inability to see that if he cannot, must not, have Ellen and the rich life of "Europe," he still has May. But having once had a vision of Ellen Olenska and her passion, May, the white and conventional counterpart of Ellen, must figure to him as the embodiment of the society that denies the vision's fulfillment. It is not so, of course. With his careful, lifelong cultivation of the sensibilities and the passions, Newland Archer has unfitted himself for passionate, devoted action. May has the last word. How rich in its suffering and incommunicable love must have been her buried life! And that very capacity to feel and to suffer serves as a cousinly and female bond between the fair lady and the dark, between May and Ellen. Archer, the object of such loves, has never been able to take the risk of either.

What a waste! Is that what one says on finishing the book? Perhaps. All that wasted motion, feeling, suffering. All that Past blotted out by change and the nice detergent of the new generation. In a sense, America *is* waste, as Edith Wharton very well knew; wasteful of its past, that greatest of resources. Yet we today, who have perhaps a nostalgia for such past times as that Edith Wharton dwells on, would do well to realize how supremely well she makes us heirs and possessors of that long-ago world. If the backward longing for the twenties Fitzgerald provoked and could not satisfy came to nothing, it may be that another novelist shall one day possess it for us, as Hawthorne possessed for us the New England of our inescapable origins. Bit by bit they will piece our American grand tour together, the novelists. We may very well not like what we find. But when we do find it—not complete but moving—we shall give Edith Wharton more of her due than she has yet received. Beyond that, and there really are things and places beyond America, we can do honor to one of the fine novels of our century. We can try to read it.

The Narrative Poem:
Novel of the Future?

I take it as axiomatic that there will be both a future and a novel—it is necessary to begin somewhere. Yet, if the future has as never before the element about it of implausibility, what of the very present, not to mention the past, for as E. H. Carr and other historians have sternly told us: no future, no past; no past, no present. One is then in the famous, or perhaps notorious, position of the usual modern fictional hero: looking for one's identity, as though one had any! Ah well, we say, very interesting, that search for the self, that Daedalusing and Joe Christmasing and Rabbit Running. How chicly Modern Man. One thing Modern Man never knows, it seems to me, is what Modern Man is. If he did, he wouldn't be, of course; he would be either a monster or God, the former, under the usual circumstances appearing the more likely chance. In any case, to look for Modern Man seems to be rather too astronautical a maneuver for a mere poet, which species, according to the "media," has long since left the human race anyhow, with what purpose in mind remains unclear; perhaps that of irritating us, on the whole a not inconsiderable object, if limited. Yet if one does not know what the poets mean by thus abandoning what we call the human race, one surely knows what the media are up to, apart from routine nastiness, simply stating what most of us think: "I don't understand this and if I did I wouldn't like it." That expresses the quintessence of philistinism, the worship of money and power, and these two things have always been preeminently the subject matter of the novel. Yet today, when money and power form the entire fabric of life, manufacture the destiny of the race, and augur well or ill for its continuance, we see the novel retreating from the sight and the subject, drawing on the one hand into a form that has been called the novel of sensibility (novels that deal in feelings, in personality, rather than action: Woolf, Proust, Joyce, etc.) and into another that I shall call the fable.

I remember infuriating an English friend not long ago by making the silly remark that ever since the English had lost the Empire they had been looking for another and had found it in sex. The English have discovered sexual passion, and it is now not only respectable but English. My friend was angry—I might add that we did not know one another very well and that in any case, in his view, sex, empire, and ideas are not playthings—he was angry, I think, not because my remark was intended as sensible, which it was not, but because there was behind it, as he knew, a double purpose: one, to pique him slightly, the other, to laugh at sexuality made dull in the contemporary English novel. My friend was an intelligent man, an Oxford classic (superb phrase. Imagine being a Yale classic!) and he knew what I meant better than I did; what he really objected to was the frivolity of my approach, my point of view. I was taking with insufficient seriousness Sex, England, empires in general, and the whole nature and destiny of man. When he pointed this out to me, classically, I had to agree. But the point remains, romantically, so what? Is that a valid objection? Surely without a very powerful undercurrent of frivolity, no literature is either delightful or lasting. Writers of fiction and drama and poetry are men and women of very strong fantasy; their imaginations tend to be both vivid and sinisterly active. When any real writer is at his best, the similarly endowed reader is likely to respond to the pretending, game-playing, fantasy-making power that communicates itself.

Let us look at some examples. Why on earth should a young man or woman today respond to Jane Austen? Are they continually making parallels between the barouche-landau and the Jaguar? between Maple Grove and White Bear Lake, between Edmund Bertram and the Princeton senior who signs up for the Peace Corps? I think not entirely. One of Jane Austen's attractive qualities for the young

lies not in any supposed correspondence between her day
and theirs but in her sense of fun and fooling, of the total
interpenetration of the serious and the absurd, the moral
and the frivolous, the ridiculous and the sublime. The young
do take themselves seriously; who knows it better than
they? They are the realest things they know, and until they
have responsibility and power, however trivial, how can
they imagine all that world of all those others? And it is
here that Jane Austen attracts them. We often ask how it
can be that a world so narrow, so apparently solipsistic, can
both fascinate and satisfy, but I daresay the perceptive
younger reader could tell us: Emma's and Elizabeth Bennett's
world is the world of the young, of the young who, fighting
their way out of the shell of self, emerge into the moral
realm and frequently do not like what they see there. Well,
then, curse God and die or learn to play in the sandbox.
See in this special, confined, and arbitrary world the delicate
patterns threaded by Emma, by Elizabeth; see how the
feminine, the individual sensibility, completed by the masculine, or intellectual, enters into love, which is the real
power, and into moral stability, which is the real gold
standard that makes mere currencies valid.

Or consider how in Conrad's *Lord Jim* youth and age,
realism and romanticism, illusion and reality confront one
another, and finally resolve either in mutual destruction or
in synthesis. Stein confronts Jim, Jim and Jewel come together, Jim in the grand gesture takes his death unflinching
and open-eyed, just as before, in blind ignominy, he had
jumped from the rail of the *Patna* into the sea of actuality.
And yet above all there is Marlowe, the sardonic, the equivo-
cal apologist who tells us tales to make the angels weep, with
one eye on the absurd larger humor of the thing and the
other eye on the tragic waste and stupidity. "In the destructive element immerse," says Stein, to the utter despair of
countless freshmen ever since. And what more does he mean
than Jane Austen meant, than Emma learned through mother wit and Mr. Knightley, than Elizabeth Bennett found in

the real Mr. D'Arcy after the unreality of her prejudices (in the root sense of that word) had dissolved? In Jane Austen, the frivolity resides in the ironic implication that everyone lives happily ever after; in Conrad, it emerges from the lucubrations of Marlowe who will not allow his over-hearers to identify themselves so narrowly with Jim that they lose the larger humor of the thing, nor to detach themselves superbly from Jim (and from Marlowe) in order to feel a proper contempt for emotion in excess of its cause and object. The young take themselves with a vast seriousness; we who are certainly older but only potentially wiser may laugh or weep at this dedication to the evidence of things not seen, as though our hard-won self-knowledge were anything better than knowing how to keep secrets.

But the writer's job is to tell secrets, and he had better have some good ones to tell before he opens his big mouth. What I have been saying may seem a far cry from the future of anything much, let alone that of the novel and the narrative poem. I gotta use words when I talk to you, as Sweeney remarked, and besides, the long way round is the shortest way with a circle. Poets and novelists try to say what's on their minds. We often wish their minds were better, perhaps, but that's another story. The point here is that modern—or contemporary—fiction seems to me to have suffered on the one hand from too advanced a technology for its moral and intellectual meaning, and on the other hand from arrested moral and intellectual development on the part of its practitioners. To put it another way: I find most modern novels to be about nothing because their authors know nothing of any interest; and I also find that nearly all of them seem difficult and obscure because they have developed formally an enormously complex computation center into which absurd or insufficient data are being fed. James is their Einstein, Proust their Rutherford, Joyce their Bohr, Faulkner their Fermi. What are we left with? Edward Teller and Werner von Braun. Or to change metaphors, the modern novelist is the inheritor of a vast estate which is entailed and all in land; he is, in fact, land-poor, but he can't get rid of it if he would, because it's against the law and nobody else wants it anyhow. I for one do not see how any modern novel can fail to seem like any six others, nor how a novelist can hope to do anything more of a formal sort until he finds something to write about that renders the whole matter of form and idiom irrelevant because it compels its own. In a word, I see the whole crisis of modern writing as one of subject.

Let me go back to the two names I dropped, the novel of sensibility and the fable. With the former we have become well acquainted, and familiarity has often bred contempt. We all know those novels and stories that are full of sensibility and no people, of delicate perceptions and no actions, of elegant phrases and metaphors and no thought, wit, or power of summation. I can hardly wait for someone to blame it all on Our Time and I don't mean *Time*, Inc. Let any such stew in that juice if he likes; it may be true, but as Henry James observed, it butters no parsnips. All right, what do we write books about—rockets? new frontiers? teenage rumbles? God forbid that I should say, if I in fact knew, which I don't. But it does seem to me that being a writer means having something to say and what one has to say is the very genius of genius. They used to tell us that form follows function; I don't know if they tell us that any more, but I keep telling myself that in literature, language and theme and image follow subject. What one has to say *is* the poem or novel and that *what* must be a person or persons doing, thinking, feeling. Any one of the three alone—any two—will not be enough. The novel of sensibility has dominated in our day because we have rejected the artificiality of plot in the old sense and have been exposed to Freud and have been engaged in expensive depth-analysis ever since. At the same time, we have known in this century more exacerbations and kicks of language than in any century since the seventeenth. Why? Is there something in the investigation of human sensibility that requires elab-

orate diction, involute syntax, fantastic rhetoric? The fact
is, all novelists of sensibility in this century have made most
violent raids on language and syntax, but have they done
much, when all is said and done, with and for that largely
passional part of the human mind, his perceptive quality?
Think how increasingly nasty, brutish, and short have become the lives of most fictional heroes and heroines; or, if
not of that sort, how intricately dull and banal. What do we
know of the remarkable Glass family except that its younger members consider themselves vastly superior to anyone
else? Sensitive, brilliant, in love with God and themselves,
they suggest a New York apartment at night. How bright,
beckoning, and tall; and in the morning how dull, mindless,
dead. What did indeed start with a desire to break the
rhetoric of melodramatic plot and stock character and to
become a full-scale investigation of the delicate and complex
sensibilities of men and women in their personal relationships, has at last become solipsism. Novels and stories do
not just dramatize this "failure to communicate" as they
say; they are in fact *about* such failure and duly fail. Solipsism is, I take it, the ultimate defeat for art, because it denies
both subject and object and hence any relation or development. It simply broods.

Of the very few escapes from this particular disaster
I would like to suggest one, and that is my other name, the
fable. God forbid that I should launch into a discussion of
myth and symbol; I want only to say that it seems to me
that a few novels of recent years have tried to escape from
sensibility by means of fable, or what I might define as that
sort of novel which combines fantasy with realism. We see
it most popularly in science fiction, but it reaches the truly
artistic and the truly fictional in such novels as William
Golding's *Lord of the Flies* and *Pincher Martin*. The essence
of the fable thus created is the fashioning of a fantastic
world in which wholly credible and realistic psychological
events take place for recognizable sorts of beings within the
framework of an action at once ambiguous and vividly, ter-

rifyingly concrete. Normally we associate the fable with satire and social commentary of whatever sort, but in the work of Golding we note that the form has moved away from the familiar type of prose fiction we have become used to, from Swift to Ray Bradbury, and has moved toward, if not allegory, then at least an intricately patterned symbolic narrative in which the language and metaphor and imagery, as well as the action, cluster about a center of ambiguous but concretely described meanings. All of this is merely to say that in such a novel as *Lord of the Flies* there is never any doubt as to what the characters say, do, think, and are, nor as to how and why they got where they happen to be, nor what is their fate. As narrative, the story utterly rejects tricks, devices, shifts in time or point of view. Events unfold naturally, in chronological sequence. What gives to the novel its resonance and scope is not only setting, situation, and action, but its use of types instead of personalities, of precise imagery and evocative language, and a genuinely different prose rhythm. Further, incident and episode seem carefully selected for two functions: furtherance of plot and action, and what I might call parallelism; that is, each incident implies a relevance forward and back in time, forward to the world of war and chaos, backward to the world of primitive savagery. This quality of resonance and parallelism is a function not only of the author's vision but of his language. One simply cannot imagine the novel of sensibility, trapped as it is within the confines of personality and Freudian psychology, developing in any such direction.

What has all of the foregoing to do with the future of narrative poetry? I hope, a great deal. In the first place, you will no doubt have gathered that I think the novel of sensibility, along with the purely realistic social document, is no longer a—shall we, alas, say it?—"viable" form. That is, I find it dull in its modern manifestations. I hasten to add that I do not at this point intend to predict the death of the novel; my purpose is to wish for a revival of narrative poetry, and having flung my pinch of spilled salt over my shoulder, here goes.

I for one do not know why people still worry so much about Alfred, Lord Tennyson; it was my impression the poor bard was dead and buried, RIP. Let us suppose that we all associated novel-reading with *Silas Marner, The Old Curiosity Shop*, and William Dean Howells. Would we think of the form with anything but a shudder? That nobody but an idiot would make such associations is clear; why therefore this inveterate reflex that connects the idea of narrative poetry with *The Idylls of the King?* Can it be, in part, that the poets are themselves to blame? I think so. They are so bloody literary! It does not seem to have occurred to many poets of this century that in writing a narrative one must use means unsuited to the lyric and reflective poem: a prosody that is primarily a vehicle, and a surface ease that invites rather than repels entrance. Does that mean *John Brown's Body*, or what I believe used to be termed "a good yarn" in, of course, a poetaster's idiom? Most of the interesting poetic narrative of this century has been written by poets who are really nineteenth-century figures—Masefield and Robinson, for example. Excellent as some of their narratives are, they do not help us in our inquiry, just as in the case of the modern novelist, Henry James is not necessarily good for what ails him. The fault is not with those stars but in ourselves, as readers and as poets or novelists.

I think, in our discussion of what a good narrative poem of the future might be like, we should start with subject, which, I trust you'll remember, I put to you as the indispensable given. But first, this brief digression. It seems to me that narrative poetry has fallen on evil days largely because the poets themselves did not see that their job was narrative. When E. M. Forster grudgingly conceded that the novel should, alas, tell a story, he was closer than he knew to the narrative technique of, let us say, Spenser. What happens in most Forster novels is pretty ridiculous; it is either

too trivial for serious concern or too melodramatic, gratui-
tously violent, for the delicate moral and social fabric that
contains it. We read Forster in spite of what happens, of the
story it tells, because we have a real concern with the people,
the moral and social states they represent, and their interre-
lationships. The story is merely a cheap glue likely to relax
when the heat is turned on. Other near-contemporaries of
Forster's looked at the matter very differently. Not Joyce,
of course, from whom all narrative writers must flee, nor
Proust, whose influence is equally pernicious. But Thomas
Mann and Joseph Conrad have other things to say and do,
and if novelists have either learned their lessons or rejected
them, the poets have not even been aware of the existence of
the school. What I am saying here is that, just as the novel
once learned from poetry, now narrative poetry must learn
from the novel; not, God help us, from "poetic" novels if
there are any such monsters, but from those novelists who
are masters of narrative, masters of symbolic action, masters of great subjects.

It is the cause, my soul: how to find a great subject
and embed it in an action so powerful that it conveys its
own symbolic meanings in the very telling. That is the crux
of the matter, and it is just there that the pitfall opens—the
great trap of allegory. For to poets, all subjects are spring-
boards into the intensity of what may seem the moral but
is often the inane. Poets as storytellers are impatient; they
want to get out of all this realistic nonsense and into the
realm of meaning. The easy way is allegory, which no one
can abide anymore now that the habit of mind is lost. The
narrative poet of the future will, I think, be a poet who
has a prose in view; not as a goal, but as a point of reference, one of several stars he may use to fix his progress
along a defined track. For example, why may a narrative
poem not use the narrative techniques of Conrad; why must
things always be told us by the presiding genius, the poet
himself? Might not *Nostromo*, for example, supply more
than one hint as to how to handle, in verse, a complex, sym-

bolic action, a large number of characters, several speakers, or narrators? Ah, you will say, I see; he wants to make the narrative poem into a versified novel. I don't think so. What I think I do mean is that now, in this era, poetry has an excellent chance to push storytelling into places it has never gone. As far as lyric, reflective, and metaphysical poetry are concerned, they have pretty well exhausted their rhetorical tradition; most poetry today is twenties free verse or psychiatric confession. Something new and good will come, it always does. But by the same token, the novel has so enslaved itself to the cult of personality that big subjects and self-revealing symbolic action are unavailable to it. Narrative poetry froze in a nineteenth-century mold. It has no rhetorical, formal, or conventional bonds to break in order to get free enough to begin.

Which leads us back to the matter of subject. What shall the epic of the future be about? Well, in the first place it won't be an epic, if by the term one means something theological, nationalistic, or linked to the supernatural; nor will it attempt that lofty view of human existence we associate with epics of the past. You will remember that it was Satan who took Christ up to a high place. Yet what on earth would be the point of writing a lengthy poem if the central action thereof were nothing much in itself? Today, of course, many a novelist in desperate search for a large subject has had increasing recourse to violence; there are obvious reasons for that, the chief being that violence can easily be made to look important. And it sells, incidentally. Most fictions keep violence close to the center of their concerns. Even Jane Austen has abductions, seductions, social disasters though of course they are in a low tone; and violence spills over constantly in the work of Dickens, as it does in that of Hardy. The world has always been a violent place, but of course what really separates the work of earlier writers from that of our own day is a conception of violence as a function of action, action toward an end that both reader and author, as well as the fictional characters, approve or reject as worthy or unworthy, in accordance with a true morality or in conflict therewith. And today who knows what such a morality is or might be? So the fictionists go on looking for new thrills, maimed debauchees, while we, exposed to their gross stimulants, react more and more feebly, like the inhabitants of *La Dolce Vita*. A Norman Mailer can make a cult of Hip and apparently believe that at the end of the mainline there's a rainbow with a crock, if not of gold, of another substance which signifies Meaning. Me, I get tired of middle-aged rebels; their particular wars have long since been won or lost, but they go on with their interminable sea-stories, not seeing that the new battles are shaping up behind their aching backs. We all hate the bourgeoisie and for good reasons, but we must face the fact that we are part of it and can not escape. Mr. Hennessey asked Mr. Dooley why it was that Benjamin Franklin was never mistaken for a waiter, whereas another ambassador of ours had been so mistaken. Mr. Dooley replied: "Perhaps becuz Binjimin Franklin niver felt like a waiter." You have to be one to know one.

Writers of serious literature are by definition split personalities. There are two tacks they can take: write about their own sources, struggles and traumas, or write their way out of them. The latter tack has been the classic way until the heyday of romanticism; in the backwash of that day we find the solipsistic fouling of one's own nest the dominant mode. What can a man find to write about? Well, I would suggest that two things in the life of the writer make his subject: experience and point of vantage. A poet or a novelist needs to know a good many things if he is going to break out of the clutches of mere sensibility; he has to have a purchase on the world of fact and men and machines, and he has to feel that world as real. The trouble has been that writers have too often felt that these matters were not real; that what had reality was feelings, reactions, relations. Hence, I think, the emphasis today on sexuality in fiction. Note that at no point in *Lady Chatterly's Lover* does Lawrence suggest that Clifford is in any way to be pitied or sympathized with though he had been brutally maimed by war, frustrated and tortured in love, and thrown on the junkpile. It has never occurred to Lawrence that here was tragedy, because he had the bee in his bonnet, and it has been buzzing in a good many otherwise sensible heads for quite some time now. There is an obscene joke that takes care of this sort of obsession and I will leave you to think of it. But the point is that Lawrence could not see his cruelty to Clifford because Clifford for him did not exist—he was not real, he simply stood for exploitation and the inhuman. That Clifford was as trapped as Connie or Mellors did not occur to him either, again because Lawrence had the arch-romantic's simpleminded view that all we need is sex or liberty or prohibition or filters or shelters or Norman Vincent Peale to be released from durance vile and translated to a higher sphere of mindless euphoria. It is an attitude no writer today can afford and which very few in the past have been able to get away with. A writer can be stupid in everything except his choice of subject, like Hemingway or Dreiser, and it does not wreck his work altogether. What does wreck it is the failure to give in to the real subject when it comes. Plenty of writers know nothing whatever about their own best quality and spend a career mixing the hopeless with the good; but the point is that when the daemon or the muse speaks, they listen and translate. It is when, as so often in the case of Lawrence, the ears are too full of one's own noisy abstractions that one loses touch, perhaps finally, with what daemon and muse have to tell. For Lawrence, when he is writing well, is a fabulist and a teller of moral fairy tales. As a thinker he is like many writers, very nearly contemptible; as an improvisator and image maker, he can be masterly, but only by fits and starts, as in "The Rocking-Horse Winner." Here a perfect sense of fable allies itself with a theme. No obsessive sexual brooding intrudes (and we must never forget that the obsessed man is mad in his obsession), no unconscious brutality to vitiate the moral view enters in, because Lawrence has stumbled upon that perfect coincidence of subject and form which every so often redeems what would otherwise be his own version of Mailer's *Advertisements For Myself*. And let us face it—only those who are well and truly hooked can react to such posturings and rantings.

Wilfrid Owen said of his poetry, "The subject of it is War, and the pity of War. The Poetry is in the pity." He knew his subject intimately, as intimately as a writer can for it killed him, and next to loving killing is the most intimate of acts. But you have to know what you are doing when you do it to make either act worthy of the name. Owen lived his subject even more closely than Conrad lived his. I do not mean to imply that in order to write about, let us say, a young girl one must undergo operations, but I do say that it would help if one had known and preferably loved at least one. Please don't anyone mention Henry James and that nonsense about his not wanting to know too much but just to imagine things, etc., etc. As a matter of fact, James was no more candid in this respect than most people; he wanted to make the art of fiction look more difficult than it obviously was for him, and as a matter of fact we know very well that he shamelessly stole from real life and modeled his more sympathetic heroines on his beloved cousin Minny Temple. He knew her, and he loved her, and Cleopatra was by no means the only female who could or can or will lay valid claim to infinite variety. James's subject was men and women and their relations, always sexual and always circumscribed by both moral and social bounds. Tennessee Williams has spent years trying to go further than James. The results are negligible.

It would seem that the truth lies in the difference between theme and subject. Owen says that his subject is war. He adds, "and the pity of War." I take this to mean that the subject is war, the pity of war the theme. The most widely publicized and praised long poems of recent years have been those of St. John Perse and Nikos Kazantzakis, and I suppose that in the case of Kazantzakis we will have to term the poem a narrative. But it would seem to me that the trouble with the work of both men is that it has no subject, only a theme or themes and hence is of wholly arbitrary length and design. Kazantzakis's *Odyssey* floats amorphously in a sea of metaphysical speculation, with neither a central action nor a particular point of vantage which the reader can grasp. Its form is vaguely picaresque, its characters have no differentiating nor humanizing features, and its episodes have at best a loosely illustrative relation to theme and are inserted apparently at random. Such a poem as "Winds" by Perse is epic rather than narrative, though of course it is neither, really, since it depends almost entirely on verbal combinations to take the place of characters and on exclamation and lofty assertion to replace action. It is not philosophical but metaphysical and full of Whitmanian ejaculations with reference to nature, reality, the future, poetry, life, and so on. In the cases of both works, one is sorely tempted to ascribe the praise showered upon them not to admiration for a great thing greatly done but because it has been done at all. Here, in this nasty materialistic, TV era, we seem to hear the pundits saying, are a couple of preposterously nonmaterialist long poems. They may not be much, but they're the best going.

The narrative poem of the future will eschew the metaphysical, the philosophical, the supernatural, the intellectual. It will have great formal integrity, plain diction, a single powerful action, and a consistent metric. It will, I think, be likely to use a historical subject for the purpose of getting at the present in order to make the future seem part of the continuum. It will, above all, combine simplicity of technique with complexity of action and point of vantage; that is, it will take a single action and involve in it representative men and women. That action will be of a sort that can reveal, as it is unfolded, its own symbolic relevance to past, present, future, and the careers of the people involved in the plot of the poem. It will be about itself in the sense that the poet will efface his personality and invent persons or voices on whose authority the story is told. It will be about itself in that it will make no attempt whatever to draw parallels, find consequences or causes, but will, on the contrary, simply present these people, this action, these themes in a totality that will be absorbed by the reader as a whole, so that later, when the reading is done, he will think not of ideas or speculations or verbal felicities but of an experience the meaning of which is a part of his life.

All very vague, high-sounding, and perhaps, in your view, impossible of achievement. But what's the use of trying to be a prophet if you don't deal with impossibilities? Just to add to the confusion, let me return to a quality I mentioned earlier as indispensable to the future writer of narrative poetry: frivolity, a sense of the actual that recognizes that nothing comes to us in its pure state because there is no such state. And here is, I think, a truth all poets should recognize: seriousness is one thing, solemnity another, and the poem that attempts scope and size must recreate the real in all its impurity. It cannot denature the real and still articulate. It must attempt many tones of voice in accordance with varying points of view and vantage, and it must attempt the larger humor of the thing, which is to say that it must accept a tragic interpretation of life. Personally, I should guess that one of the themes of such a narrative poetry will almost of necessity be the use and misuse of power. Another of many possibilities will be the theme of money, its function in human relationships and in the manipulation of reality. And lest this sound too formidable, too social-documentary, let me put it another way. The novel of sensibility, the feminine aspect of fiction, has dominated in recent years. It's angst angst all the way, with an occasional Jewish kicker for the tolerant trade as well as for local color. Well and good, but what I think the new supreme fiction needs is a strong injection of masculine moral and intellectual vitality. Don't ask me where this is to come from; presumably from a strongly moral, intel-

lectual, and masculine mind. In any case, I do not see how
the fiction is to balance the frivolous with the tragic unless
it contains the moral and the intellectual passions, passions
surely as real and as exciting as the sexual or the simply
nervous. More Conrad, less Tennessee Williams; less Marianne Moore, more Owen, Crane, Yeats. Poetry today, like
fiction, is of three sorts, the coy, the camp, and the confessional. Start with Robert Lowell and you end with Anne
Sexton; start with Stevens and you end with Charles Tom-
linson. I am not asking for an era of poetic jocks, nor for a
Tolstoy come to judgment; just for a certain widening of
the range, a greater inclusiveness, a complementing of the
feminine sensibility with the masculine mind.

It may well be asked at this point: why seems it so particular with narrative poetry? Wouldn't all this suit the
novel just as well? My only answer is, It would, but it won't.
That is, I don't myself believe the novel, bound as it is to
tradition and to commerce, is in as favorable a position to
cut loose. Narrative poetry as we have known it in the past
decades has been too often the province of inferior poets, a
province which has seemed to most poets of stature exhausted and barren. Lyrical poetry has been the thing, or if
not lyrical at least short. Compression, ironic understate-
ment, frenetic and elliptical imagery—by these signs do we
know a modern poem. Curious how the novel has moved in
a similar direction; bit by bit it jettisons baggage in order
to keep the old bourgeois epic afloat. It can go a great deal
further in that direction, too. But poetry has gone as far
that way as it can, and, for all I can see, only a few Beats
have tried to wrench it off course. Yet their devices are only
devices, mostly crude and wholly solipsistic. They don't
know anything and they have no vitality—only tics and
spasms. What it all boils down to is that a modern poet
who writes a narrative poem must be first a poet and second
a teller of tales. Events, the real world, and a moral universe
of some sort must all have existence for him, and he must
have a rhetoric to go with all these. I am fully aware that

rhetoric is a dirty word in this day of poems that sound like
See the dog. The dog is Spot. Come Spot, etc. If you think
that's a parody, look at any little magazine. No, rhetoric is
indispensable and at this point only the poets are in a position to find it. Let them steal narrative techniques as such
wherever those techniques are effectively deployed, but let
them remember that it is language that will give the story
life, and language is their business—that and moral vision.
Let our narrative poet say, Out upon Ezra Pound and a
murrain upon the language of William Carlos Williams.

Finally, a word on science and technology, although
as far as I am concerned Wordsworth said it. If Sir Charles
Snow were only right, how simple a matter it would be,
that matter of two cultures. But there are I fear many more
cultures than he instances, with the promise or threat of
more to come. Good say I; that is what poets and novelists
are for, to live and breathe in that multiplicity of worlds
and to assimilate it to themselves and give it back to men
somehow made tolerable and exciting rather than menacing
and dull. Why should an electronic engineer respond to
"Aesthétique du Mal" or a poet to hydrostatics or the man
in the street to either? Unless these things affect him nearly
he cannot, and it is idle to say that they do affect him nearly.
In certain cases the results of science have an impact on our
lives, just as do teenage rumbles in Brooklyn. They are part
of our time, they make the time, they are all bound up in
what we call reality, but they need not in all cases seize the
imagination. If they did, there would be no need for art because we would all of us, in our daily living, be making a
work of imagination out of raw experience. We do not and
cannot thus imagine; we want, those of us who have the desire, to have our artists do that for us, and some, like Hart
Crane, have made the attempt. Let our narrative poet of the
future live in his time and assimilate to himself as much
of that time as he can. He cannot avoid what is uppermost
in the concerns of men and he need not go to Cal Tech to
understand about it what is worth understanding. He is not

out to manipulate nature or reality but to understand it, to come to terms with it, to make peace with it. Or if necessary, to indict and condemn it. John Dryden learned what he learned, and it was considerable, by listening to people talk shop. So did Dickens and Tolstoy and Kipling. Our narrative poet will follow their example and will not spend his time talking to other poets, critics, litterateurs, and lion tamers. They have nothing to tell him because they do nothing, and he will want to be listening in quarters where money is made and power generated and used. Those quarters are not necessarily in national capitals or industrial board rooms but as often in suburbs late on Friday or Saturday night, at cocktail parties, on planes, commuting trains, and in bars and restaurants. Our poet is in for a good deal of boredom, to be sure, but he is better off there than in graduate school or the *hungry i*. As long as he knows that he is a poet, that the men of power are what they obviously are and that he is there to listen and absorb for later use—then he can forget how many cultures there are because to all intents and purposes, they are he. Techniques, special knowledge, learning; these are not for him because they get in the way. But the men who have them, who use them and are used by them, they are his meat and his subject. All he requires is an appetite and genius. John Milton was a fool to Richard Hooker and Norman Vincent Peale, as was Dante to Thomas Aquinas and Bishop Sheen.

Edward Thomas and the Real World

The visible world exists. Violated, despoiled, lacerated —the sensible world takes charge and a poet ignores or wrongs that world at the peril not only of his life but of his immortal soul, because, believe it or not, the secret is Incarnation, and we attend to it when we feel the world as a presence that compels our assent, in spite of another world of abstraction.

We must attend, and attention is everything. Attention in action consists for present purposes of three actors: the poet, the poem, and the reader. Obviously when each does the job assigned, something like incarnation—a "model" of incarnation as we might put it today—comes to pass: the word is made flesh and dwells among us, for a time only, but returning whenever the complex act occurs and the three are gathered together. But lest that sound too pompous and New Testamentary, I come back to this odd trinity I've devised and begin with the act of attention in the poet.

Robert Penn Warren tells us, in his poem "Court-Martial," that "the world is real, it is there." Not, mind you, here. OUT there. Inescapably other, wholly resistent to pathetic fallacy in whatever guise, the "sensible" world at once defies the poet and seduces him, always escaping but always There. No wonder so-called mystical poetry is often such a fraud, however "honorable" the poet's intention: he is the man who sees visions that he takes to be revealed truth, real gardens with imaginary angels, and would tell the world that his metaphor is fact. Such a poet does not pay proper attention, listens to himself too closely and only too distantly to the world that is there. He is, finally, a poet who confronts "the nothing that is not there / And the nothing that is" with a point of view so distracted that he can see

only the glare of opinion. He does not see what is There; he
will set himself first and not really look, not pay attention.

> They were more dexterous and much more dangerous than
> when they pretended they were robbers or Indians; and
> now their make-believe was really serious to them. You
> found it funny or called it silly at your peril. Credulity had
> been renamed faith. Each childish adult determinedly bet
> his life and staked his sacred pride on, say, the Marxist's
> ludicrous substance of things only hoped for, or the Chris-
> tian casuist's wishful evidence of things not so much as
> seen. Faiths like these were facts. They must be taken into
> account; you must do the best you could with them, or in
> spite of them.

Thus Colonel Ross ruminates in Cozzens's *Guard of Honor*.
It is a state, as he puts it, of the "boy's unwarranted entertainment and unfounded terror in a state of things systematically misunderstood." The error, of course, derives
from a preference for illusion over reality, and if we can
from time to time agree with Conrad that under certain circumstances illusion can preserve, nourish, and sustain, we
must equally recognize that the man who takes metaphor
for actuality and the sensible world for the neutral back-
ground against which he may shine is indeed a dangerous
creature, beyond help and beyond control or trust.

Now none of this is to say that poetry must be about
nature or whatever. The suburbs are full of nature-lovers,
but there is a not inconsiderable difference between mild
bird-watching and really finding "splendor in the grass,
glory in the flower." Where, as a matter of fact, do we find
splendor and glory? Who finds and proclaims and celebrates
them? Swinburne observed that all criticism was vicious
that did not consist of "the noble art of praising," but for
the act of praise a poet must be found worthy, and he can
only be found so if he can shut up and listen, can develop
ears and eyes, and "a heart that watches and receives."

Now I have to grant that none of all this means a thing

if our poet lacks genius, a very rare, very peculiar way with words and with words' capacity to discover all kinds of things, visible and invisible. Our poet must have double vision, a knowledge of inner and outer weather and the relation between the two. He has to take his own readings frequently, which means that he must have some real understanding of his own best subject—it is doubtful that a poet can have more than two subjects—and either may be the antisubject, or parody of the real heart of the matter. All too frequently it is this antisubject which critics take for the true mirror of nature. Lacking any interest in the poem itself, they substitute for that interest a passion for the grand synthesis, the key to all mythologies, a transcendental vision which annihilates the poem, because a poem is a concrete object in a concrete world.

The legend goes that Frost inspired, if that's the word, Edward Thomas sufficiently so that Thomas turned from prose to poetry, having of course never considered the possibility before. One need only know something of Thomas's own work to read the story differently: he found in the presence of Frost and his poetry something that made his own muse say to him: "I've been trying to tell you this all along and you listen but don't dare. Now you will dare." The most interesting thing about Thomas's "drop into poetry," as Dickens's Silas Wegg puts it, is the curious difference between the two poets' feel for language and its movement. We would expect Frost at this stage to be more "sophisticated," more assured, yet in fact Thomas's language has far less of the archaic, indeed of the near-sentimental, than does Frost's. And brief though the time was of Thomas's growth and flowering, before the war killed him he had perhaps done all in that mode that he could have; what should have come after would have had to be other and very different. He had found a couple of tunes that his words would fit: one of them, the tune of "As the Team's Head-Brass," the other of, say "Lights Out." Song and meditation are the poles; the poems range in between them. Frost's tune he himself describes pretty accurately, and the difference between, say "The Witch of Coos" and "Spring Pools" is one of expansion and contraction rather than one of a wholly other song. The "wild tune" he speaks of may become more or less wild in a given poem; the degree of dramatic irony and of humor in a given poem determines the degree of wildness. With Thomas, the tune comes closer to Elizabethan song on the one hand, and on the other to the use of a syntax that approaches the conversational and *suggests* prose rather than uses it.

At the heart of Thomas's poetry lies the paradox: love and death. Nowhere does this emerge more powerfully than in "As the Team's Head-Brass," because there we see a poem which deliberately brings together all of the themes Thomas had up to this time been obsessed by. The structure of the poem is thematic and metaphorical, like the best of Frost. Thomas provides three intellectual and concrete clusters of meaning and images in the lovers, the fallen elm, the team of plough horses. And of course, there are the voices of the ploughman and of Thomas, and the voice of that third person, the poet Thomas. The observer, the poet Thomas, takes a position in the middle distance so that he can see, if not all, then most of what happens in the visible world; he does not even speculate on meaning or possibility. At one point, the Thomas who is "in" the poem says "Everything / Would have been different. For it would have been / Another world." Immediately the ploughman adds: "Ay, and a better, though / If we could see all all might seem good." The lovers will come out of the wood almost immediately after this interchange; up to this point the talk has been of killing and wounds; the elm, dead and felled, makes a seat for the speaker, and as the ploughman comes round with the team, he pauses for a word or two. Everything in the poem comes together: love, war, death, wounds, endurance, and the not-quite defeat of hope. The poet watches at the very end "the clods crumble and topple over / After the ploughshare and the stumbling team."

How to do everything at once! Without making an uproar. One might spend an hour just looking at the use of sound and its repetitive patterns in the poem—not to mention the halts and rushes of the metric and line structure. Here in fact we have what Frost claims for his own music. For one reader, at any rate, the claim justifies itself more fully in this poem by Thomas than any one of Frost's that comes to mind. But that only underlines the point that seems central here: Frost and Thomas not only live outside the movement of modernism in their time; they create a third world of poetry that certainly has its roots deep in "the tradition" but which owes nothing whatever to either the symbolist or the imagist-expressionist modes that dominated—or were to dominate—the poetry of the next forty years. Neither man had any aesthetic ideas or aims, in the first place; they made no conscious or unconscious analogies with science and technology, which in effect was the underlying imperative of Pound's "make it new." Thomas, if he had said anything at all, would simply have said, "Make it. Don't talk about it."

The heart of the matter is the matter of metaphor, and the underside of that matter is movement. Metaphor in motion. The something seen in its passage, caught for an instant, set down. Nothing new of course. And Pound himself recognized that peculiar poetic essence when he saw it, as he did in the case of Frost and others. What Pound and the Imagists did that could have no blessing on it was to set up idols and worship them: they took fact for truth, objects for incarnation. They thought that one could *create* a living language and a new world of art out of icons and feminine endings. In other words, they thought if they could make the theory, God would give them practice. Then they forgot about the senior partner. All of which is a rather flip, generalized cynicism. But it does not interfere with the truth that in losing sight of, and the capacity for, metaphor, they lost sight of the fundamental idea of a poem as metaphor, the poem as an imitation of an action, made of words in motion. There has surely been no poetry more "difficult" than Pound's; that is what makes it so attractive to so many, but one feels that too often we are being given by the critics a highly respectable and rational analysis of what is both egocentric and nutty—not to say at times fraudulent. One cannot of course blame a poet for his critics or readers, and God knows that symbolism has its nuts, frauds, and creeps, too. There is no question here of traditionalist versus modernist; only of two innate convictions about the true nature of the source of poetry.

The source is the visible world. How many times do we have to violate that world to know that it exists? Symbolism tries to bypass it by means of selecting from it only its epiphenomena and by making of them patterns of irrationality and abstraction which become formulaic; i.e., abstract a phenomenon from sensory reality, remove its physical features and effects, then equate it with another phenomenon identically treated. Voilà: *Le bateau ivre.* Or most of *The Waste Land.* Now only a powerful mind and imagination can perform anything at all in true poetry of any kind and provenience, but in symbolism the usually fatal tendency is for the rational faculty, wholly in the service of its symbolist theory, to apply itself without letup to the manufacture and extension of symbolist structures or constructs. The best explication of this manner and mode that comes to mind is Hart Crane's letter to Harriet Monroe explaining the matter and meaning of the process that makes up his "At Melville's Tomb." "The statement was interesting but tough," as Huck Finn observed of another structure. Why? Because in all such matters we are dealing with expressiveness, expressive form and expressive language and meaning. Now Hart Crane and Arthur Rimbaud were men of genius whose work remains splendid at moments in spite of theory and practice, because at their best times they wrote against their theory or their commitment, and from that conflict came another element. The redeemer? Compare "At Melville's Tomb" with "The Broken Tower" and you have the answer: "There are nine and sixty ways of constructing tribal lays / And every single one of them is right," says Kipling, and he ought to know.

Metaphor knows nothing of the expressive: the metaphorical poet is John Crowe Ransom's "poet nearly anonymous." "The world is real. It is there," to go back to the beginning. All right: so there it is. Now don't just stand there; go there and do something with it that will bring it home to men who can receive it. And return it, both parties the better for the trip. Which is what Frost means when he says "Earth's the right place for love. I don't know where / It's likely to go better."

A poet, however great, is not God. He cannot say "Behold I make all things new" and make it stick. Neither can he make a tradition: he can use only what is There— Out There, not in here. Swift had the true fable, of the Spider and the Bee. Poetry is not made of spun guts or failed feeling. Metaphor makes it: "The horses started and for the last time / I watched the clods crumble and topple over / After the ploughshare and the stumbling team." That ends the poem which began as the head-brass "flashed out on the turn." It does not flash at the end. The lovers have left the wood, and the ploughman and Thomas himself have to go their ways—"stumbling" along with the more docile beasts. You call this depressing? Exaltation rather is the final effect; love, war, death, endurance, courage, faith—and none discussed, only given. Above all, perhaps, the poet lets the poem speak, and neither pushes opinions nor sums up. And he does not set a group of images alongside an "idea" and say, look; things equal to the same thing are equal to each other. He makes a scene with people and other creatures and a war and a particular time and place, shows what happens, then leaves. No big effects; everything on the scale of the ordinary. The extraordinary derives from Thomas's concrete particularity of "rendering" and the careful selection of parts, equally carefully articulated and shown. A symbolist like Crane, in a poem such as "At Melville's Tomb," uses association as his method: every object or natural phenomenon becomes something else before it finds a place: the analogy is with expressionistic film and jazz improvisation, whether conscious or unconscious or both on Crane's part I cannot say. But what his own *explication de texte* (and how seriously did Crane take it?) shows to us—apart from his wish to be thought a "careful" poet—is that anyone can play that game of the random element as a higher logic. Crane was of course a superb formalist, but when he unzipped, disaster followed, as witness most of "The Bridge"; but when he puts mind and imagination into form as in "The Broken Tower," we see what symbolism can do. As theory, it is nothing; in practice it becomes a kind of power only when it serves metaphor. The truth is of course that metaphor contains—in every sense of the verb—the symbolic energy. Symbolism would escape this world and the concrete; metaphor so loves the world that it insists on a return to the world around us, however high or far the fancy would try to fly. Reverse William Carlos Williams's apothegm "No things but in ideas." Then restore it. Thomas wrote as the last line of "Swedes": "This is a dream of Winter, sweet as Spring." How do you get there from a pile of turnips? He gets there.

Poetry and—Religion?

Perhaps I should begin with an apology for using the word at all. Is there such a thing as religion—or belief—anymore? Superstition, si. Belief, no. It is not, I think, a matter of temperament nor of "the time"; rather, one of affluence and hedonism, as well as racial and cultural diversity. Religion in the old sense, and of course one means Christianity, simply does not work. Perhaps more to the point, Christians don't. Transcendental meditation *does* work, we are told by the meditators; the fact that it is both solipsistic and merely palliative of what ails them suggests that for most people Christianity does not work because one cannot believe—not IN it, but IT. The process of gutting all creeds has gone on for a long time, and nowhere can we see the results more plainly than among the poets, most notably those who have had their religious roots or conversions but had to backslide in the face of the evidence.

The evidence in most cases has been facts. New England started the whole thing. Surely no other region of the United States has, over the past century and a half, provided a larger portion of the gross national product of up-country metaphysics, cracker-barrel mystics, self-appointed hierophants and prophets. Ralph Waldo Emerson is largely to blame, of course. When Puritanism took the veil and the Unitarian myopic became Chief Seer, it was all up with visions and the Incarnate Word. Not to mention the poetry that they inspired. Jones Very's crazy antics appalled Emerson; he was not a Samuel Johnson who could feel what Kit Smart was up to. But then, Johnson was a devout Christian and Emerson—well, Emerson was a hierophant. A hierophant with the metaphysical appetite and a vestigial love for the Incarnate—not Word, but words. But if it hadn't been Emerson, it would have been Bronson Alcott or someone else of the same name. Christianity had been Puritan, and no growing, complex, and polymorphous society can abide restraints born of total agreement as to the nature of first and last things. Ancestral and parental authority estranges the young and breeds disaffection in their elders. Now add pop Freudianism to the brew and belief in anything becomes an act of will, not a movement of the spirit. Indeed, the revulsion against creed in favor of the embrace of euphoria renders belief both superfluous and archaic. Poets know this better than anyone, it would seem; at least, they have been explicit about it, as witness much or all of John Berryman's late work. It is not that orthodoxy must command if a poet is to win both belief and a *Divine Comedy* for our time; rather, our poets often seem to use the poetry as a confessional, with the reader not so much priest as tape recorder. One hears the poet rehearsing his backslidings and accusations and world-sorrows, not as agonies but deformities, the nastier for being so perfectly understood by the poet. The compulsion to explain oneself, and thereby explain away, becomes the confessional. Not of course the general confession of the liturgy but a personal, agonized, and too frequently self-deceptive tirade aimed at a kind of exculpation: "I suffered. I was there." No question of belief, of prayer, or desire for reform in which both will and belief must participate. Poetic forms must shore up the sick soul that it may at least keep unbelief from committing murder.

No one who reads poetry for pleasure and profit is likely to concern himself overmuch with the particular convictions of particular poets; if those convictions seem to "work" as far as poems are concerned, one is more than content. That anyone, least of all a poet, should have what is vulgarly known as a "philosophy of life" would seem irrelevant, if not downright harmful, to any position or attitude or commitment describable as "poetic." Religion has usually meant commitment to a body of doctrine, a faith, or a confession. Under the circumstances of past and present New England, this must mean some Christian denomination, always assuming that Unitarianism is Christian. I do not think that under present conditions such an approach will serve. Here it seems better to try to find in the poets and poetry under discussion some kind of genuinely religious commitment, at least to the extent that one can find in the work at issue evidence of a movement toward, about, or away from some center that can be called equally doctrinal and spiritual in the religious-Christian senses. And from the beginning—if by the beginning one means the nineteenth century—we are in trouble.

We begin, inevitably, with everyone's favorite whipping boy, the Protestant ethic, or Puritan disaster. Is this not what most of us mean when we speak of New England and religion, quite ignoring the fact that for one hundred years New England has been preponderantly Roman or Irish (now Italian) Catholic? Yet there is something in it, if only the fact—and it is a fact—that Puritanism existed, still exists, and has marked Roman Catholicism (though not Anglo) indelibly, as these things go. Yet like all movements of attitudes or passions, as history views them, they loom largest to our consciousness when they are actually in decline. It is the aftereffects, the backwash, so to speak, of which we, as spectators primarily, become most aware. It is so with the poetry. Who, after all, are the greatest New England poets of the "modern" era? Emily Dickinson, E. A. Robinson, Robert Frost. The case for them as true New Englanders and poets of the first rank is not open to serious question. Looking before and after them, we are lost. For my purposes in this investigation, these three will form the essential set of touchstones, the latter two most obviously as nearest in time to the chronological period under investigation. And can any one of them be called in any meaningful way "religious"?

Oh, of course, Dickinson—in the sense that the Jesuits can claim Joyce now that he is not here to object! But Frost, sly broken-field runner that he is, evades the ontological questions at the points where they might intersect with religious opinion, and Robinson is far nearer to a kind of Unitarian ethic than to a theological position. Just what do we mean? In the case of Dickinson, we mean, I think, that she jettisoned almost entirely orthodoxy and doctrine in order to be free to make images of her inner thought and passion. Puritanism—the Protestant ethic—gave her a tune and a few spare instruments. She made up the words out of a worn-out theological vocabulary and a wholly fresh look at the little world she knew. It is, of course, the besetting sin of New England artists, to go "woods queer" as they still say of trappers and hunters, to become eccentric; occasionally, not to put too fine a point upon it, to go mad. Jones Very is an excellent example of the type, though in good New England style he committed himself to the asylum rather than give others trouble.

The villain of the piece, then, is neither John Calvin nor Cotton Mather nor Jonathan Edwards but Emerson, who had the temerity, the presumption, to consider Jones Very mad. But Emerson was less one for action than for intuitive, ill-considered statement: "Good is positive. Evil is merely privative, not absolute," or "He [Christ] said, in this jubilee of sublime emotion, 'I am divine. Through me, God acts; through me, speaks. Would you see God, see me; or see thee, when thou also thinkest as I now think.'" What can any religious order or dogma do with such ideas? The matter is so simple for Emerson, so much a matter of the individual's simple vision and simple choice. If many of those who listened to Emerson were themselves of a reforming and liberal constitution, there were more importantly those of a hard and driving acquisitive temper who seized on Emerson's comfortable words as their hunting license. For the poets and artists such words could bring only alarm on the one hand or blessed release on the other, for as poet one was either bound to pursue truth and the ultimate questions in the old way, or in the new turn inward where a rarer truth was to find.

Surely the matter is one of romanticism in its voyages of discovery. From rebellion to independence, from independence to weariness to boredom to despair. From self-dependence to self-absorption to solipsism. Wordsworth, in *The Prelude*, wrote more wisely than he could himself bring to fruition in his own later life and work, but we do not condemn, for he always kept the "anchor in the senses" in the best of his work, and after turning inward, turned out again to the world of men and the heart's affections. It is only later, in Arnold and Tennyson, that we see the heartache and the despair which increasingly will turn the poet away from his fellows and they from him ("But fly our paths, our feverish contact fly") as each man alone tries to find Emerson's god in himself. What he in fact is to find is a chamber of horrors, and the poets will not hesitate to describe the contents and occupants.

Is it the chicken or the egg? Did the poets, like most sensitive, imaginative, and intelligent people, suddenly find that science has rendered god obsolete? Or, having found God obsolete, did they let science or whatever move into the breach? Have they become so concerned with the simultaneous cultivation of physical nature and the individual self that there is no need for God? That would appear to be the course romanticism took. Whitman has no need for God—only for vague *camerados* and for leisure to loaf and invite his soul, and Thoreau needs only the woods and his soul. God is in one or the other or both or neither, but it really doesn't matter as long as one—or you and I and anyone—feels reverence and pleasure and so forth. The step to Hemingway is inconsiderable. Yet to read the poetry of the modern age is to sense that there is far more to it than that. Here is no rejoicing at delivery from bondage, from Old Nobodaddy:

> Meanwhile, we do no harm, for they
>   That with a god have striven,
> Not hearing much of what we say,
>   Take what the god has given;

> Though like waves breaking it may be
> Or like a changed, familiar tree
> Or like a stairway to the sea
>   Where down the blind are driven.

This is Robinson. He does not rejoice. We are all, he said, like children in a nursery "trying to spell God with the wrong blocks." And Frost: "We dance round in a ring and suppose / But the Secret sits in the middle and knows." When all allowances are made for characteristic manner and feeling, we still see that both poets reserve judgment, they wait, they strike toward a supposed center from the outer edges, then, as the rumor of the Secret reaches them, they wait and listen. Above all, they do not make holy noises nor try to keep up their spirits with liturgical, mystical, or poetic echoes. If there must be a God, he had better not be invented. He must Be. Meanwhile we must take what He has given, whether or not He is the one who gives it.

Such a rigorous approach is not for all, poets or others. There can be a religion of art, as Arnold recommended and Wallace Stevens tried to demonstrate, but it can never engage the whole man nor many men. There can equally be neopaganism, a religion compounded of art, sensual life, and nature, as in the best work of Phelps Putnam:

> In Springfield Massachusetts I devoured
> The mystic, the improbable, the Rose . . .
> I had my banquet by the beams
> Of four electric stars which shone
> Weakly into my room, for there . . .
> Was the incarnate star
> Whose body bore the stigma of the Rose . . .

For all the surface lyricism in Putnam's best poems, notably "Ballad of A Strange Thing," we feel the death underneath, the terrible isolation that comes with the dawn and hangover. "In the real dark night of the soul," says Scott Fitzgerald (and he knew), "it is always three in the morning." He might have added, as one feels sure he wished us to add, the line from the song whose title he has here borrowed, "We've danced the whole night through." Putnam knows that dark night and writes it out: from independence to self-abandonment to loneliness and despair. Where can the heart abide? The foreigners come in and take the land away from us. They afflict us with their wars and their sophisticated curses, we who were born free and innocent, with the capacity for the fullest life and the most superb vitality. With a characteristically modern accent and New England wryness, Putnam writes his Mutabilitie Cantos. New England, which was pagan innocence; youth, which was joy and companionship; love which was sensual delight—all die. And there is nothing after.

Who will call such an attitude childish or inadequate? Did Putnam himself not die of it? And Edna Millay? "Man is in love and loves what vanishes; / What more is there to say?" Thus Yeats. Other poets, contemporaries of Putnam, would try to remake both a poetics and a religion from the ground up and shore fragments against their ruins, but when the New England poets attempt such maneuvers, they tend to sound either hysterical or insincere, and in any case, the usual Roman Catholic gambit they attempt in order to gain the victory over chaos usually strikes one as an effort of the will rather than a descent of the dove:

> These are the tranquillized *Fifties*,
> and I am forty. Ought I to forget my seedtime?
> I was a fire-breathing Catholic C.O.,
> and made my manic statement . . .

Thus Robert Lowell in *Life Studies*, half a life and a religion away from *Lord Weary's Castle* and *The Mills of The Kavanaughs*. Does he tell us in these lines that it was all delusion, the sick recourse of a sick mind? Is it he or the time or the belief that is out of joint? Or all of them? or perhaps none, and the poems of *Life Studies* simply record change, gradual desolation of spirit and sense? In the first poem of that book, "Beyond the Alps," Lowell seems to have got no further with it than the Arnold of "The Scholar-Gypsy," though he exhibits all the symptoms of those ills that Arnold warned his man to fly. It is the history of a malaise, relentlessly catalogued in the sincerity of strong feeling and the perfect memory of total recall. Lowell, certainly the inventor of the confessional mode, absolutely rejects the speculative, the philosophical or metaphysical questioning that Robinson may have finally killed off in its nineteenth-century form in "The Man Against the Sky." Religion or the quest for transcendence can now have no meaning; it is no longer a problem; its questions are no longer questions at all but circular arguments starting nowhere, their source an individual craving, their end individual peace. But the mind changes, desire moves and can not rest:

> the blear-eyed ego kicking in my berth
> lay still, and saw Apollo plant his heels
> on terra firma through the morning's thigh . . .
> each backward, wasted Alp, a Parthenon,
> fire-branded socket of the Cyclop's eye . . .

The poet lies under a curse. Try what he will—lust as he may after strange women, gods, and images—he comes back to his father's house, or to his grandfather's, "the family graveyard in Dunbarton." The mills of the Kavanaughs grind exceeding small and the poet, his "blear-eyed ego" destructively thrashing about in the old family properties, loves and hates simultaneously the heritage, the money, the decadence, and the memories: "ought I to forget my seedtime?" It is a question only the poet can ask, only the man can answer.

It was not always so. It was not always expected—demanded—that the poet jettison the past and walk the freer for the lighter load. Have we Emerson again to blame? Emerson and Whitman? In any case, the poets born in the nineteenth century who came to poetic maturity in the twentieth, Robinson and Frost, were still sure enough of themselves and their craft to take for granted both their own personal identities and their own poetry as valid entities; they did not feel it necessary to ask the questions, Who am I and what am I doing here? They put it this way: Granted myself and this world, where do we go from here? And ancillary to this question they have left us statements about what it is like down here, with a few footnotes on hell.

> And we who delve into beauty's lore
> Know all that we have known before
> Of what inexorable cause
> Makes time so vicious in his reaping.

Robinson in "For a Dead Lady," a poem wrung out of him on the death of his mother, lays the whole thing on the line. There is no more to be said, and we must all go on, go on and act as if. Significantly, in his foreword to Robinson's posthumously published *King Jasper*, Frost quotes some lines from Robinson's "The Dark Hills," emphasizing "As if the last of days were fading and all wars were done." The tone that dominates in this poem is irony, cosmic and tragic, undergirding a view of reality so stern and tough that few readers take to it. It has no Dostoevskian sentimentality about it, nor does it concede anything to Emersonian imperatives. Both Robinson and Frost were very tough men and poets. They had their foibles and their delicacies and their sentimentalities, but when they wrote their poems they were ruthless and alone. Unlike Lowell, for example, they feel free to speculate openly and broadly about certain large questions. They ask nature to stand and deliver: are you good, bad, or indifferent? They tell us, "Home is the place that when you go there, they have to take you in," or "He may by contemplation learn / A little more than what he knew / And even see great oaks return / To acorns out of which they grew." It is a poetry of statement, based on metaphor or dramatic situation, in which the speaker of the poem wrestles with possibilities and facts, with natu-

ral laws and human nature, always recognizing that there
may be more—or less—than meets the eye: "But when was
that ever a bar / To any watch they keep?"

The contemporary poet, in his search for verities, must
go inward, or at any rate he does so. Find what you are
yourself, the poet seems to tell himself; then and only then
can the real world begin, made from scratch, "lock, stock
and barrel / Out of his bitter soul." That of course is
Yeats speaking, not today's poet, who has first to find a
soul and in any case means *his* soul, not Yeats's mansoul.
The search for personal identity must preclude any other;
no meaning outside without meaning within. Is it any
wonder that much of this poetry is sick, that its setting or
its theme involves the psychiatric ward, the clinical confessional, the hospital? Lowell here sets the tone, pace and
pattern, followed closely by his disciple Ann Sexton, whose
poems seem not so much props against chaos as fever charts,
day-to-day briefings on how it is with the weather of the
psyche. In such poetry, the religious frame of mind is
impossible and can only be rarely and obliquely adverted
to as nostalgia or withheld blessing. The age of revolution
and atheism is long gone; religion seems less curse than
accident, something you have from being raised Catholic
or from falling into it like a pit. One either outgrows it or
grows into it. The true constant, the absolute, is Lowell's
"blear-eyed ego" warring with the sick soul.

The early sort of atheistical or rebellious credos found
their best utterance in E. E. Cummings's earlier poetry, in
which religion figures as the villain, the senile Nobodaddy
of the "Cambridge ladies who live in furnished souls" or the
sterile, androgynous god best symbolized by the "castrated
pup." Yet Cummings comes closer than any poet of modern
New England to a religion of humanity, to a worship of love
that though at times fulsome, at best retains a reverence
for life which can create holiness, the spirit of Blake's "I
forgive you and you forgive me / Throughout all eternity,"
a feeling and a conviction that is sufficiently rich and rigor-

ous to deserve the term "religious." Note how, in "A man who had fallen among thieves" Cummings, starting with the parable of the Good Samaritan, dramatizes and makes holy the spirit of redemption through humility and awe. One could almost say that the poem demonstrates the working of the Holy Spirit in the way in which the anonymous "I" of the poem simply goes about his work of mercy, of healing and transfiguration, without thought or hesitation. What Cummings can do best—and so often—is to convey a sense of the sacred, the ineffable, in the small things that compose daily life. If there is an Emersonian streak in Cummings, it is less tendentious and abstract and cloudy; Cummings does not plague us with mere opinion nor with rhetoric. Even his hatred seems holy—a Christlike scourging of the chamber of commerce. Life with a blessing on it gives the best of these poems their quality. That sort of life and quality is what later poets seem to strive for but, trapped in the search for individual self, both blessing and life seem to fly their feverish contact: "I keep no rank or station. / Cured, I am frizzled, stale and small." For Lowell, the world has to remake itself in him daily.

Might it be said with justice that to many moderns the notion that one can "go it alone," so to speak, in this accidental world is repugnant? "That was a way of putting it," says Eliot, speaking of the earlier rhetoric and the cosmic questions of a simpler age. It WAS—it can be no longer. Again, the poet sees that the questions no longer mean anything; therefore the answers are irrelevant. Yet he comes later to the conviction that both questions and answers may be meaningful and central once again if the former are put in different language and contexts, and the answers given from a rediscovered source. At any rate, "for us there is only the trying."

Thus far we have found little or no evidence of a truly religious poetry in modern New England, yet we must not therefore assume that in the poets whom we are considering the religious sense is dead. On the contrary, the appetite for the transcendental (if not the transcendent) which has long characterized New England remains; sometimes in the form of the still exacerbated conscience, of total war on religious perversions, of search for something to believe in. As we have seen, the characteristic introspection of the Puritan has turned quite naturally to a rootless solipsism and self-scrutiny. Where the Puritan looked into himself for reason, motive, and understanding, the modern poet frequently looks into the snake pit of the soul, if only to list and describe the fauna he thinks he sees there. Any inward gaze may mistake sincerity for honesty. Just as the evil old Puritan in the legend could see only the beam in his brother's eye though he gazed never so hard into his own, so the modern poet in inviting his sick soul may discover only what it pleases or flatters him to find. Sick people are more interesting than well—up to a point. Suffering can be such a bore, particularly if one goes on about it, just as the Puritan compulsion to analyze one's religious state became finally tedious and then pernicious. It ceased to be honest, only sincere, like the true confessions of an advertising executive. To be thoroughly honest in one's poetry—that, as Yvor Winters has pointed out in the case of Robinson, is not only the sign of genius but also that sign least likely to attract the attention or favor of critics. Neither Frost nor Robinson in their poems went in for the self-display or the pyrotechnics of a Pound, say, and of course the themes they treated were as unfashionable as the forms and textures they employed. Frost seems to have an immediate appeal because of his apparent simplicity and the natural detail that one can easily believe is one's own experience of a lost youth and a dear, dead, pastoral world. It is of course all a trap. Other poets— R. P. T. Coffin is a good example—set out to follow in Frost's footsteps, only to lose themselves. We readers become entrapped in the snare of our own stock responses to what we think is "nature poetry." Lionel Trilling certainly found that out when, at the Frost birthday dinner, he tried to tell the assembly what Frost's poetry was like. Always, for Frost as for Robinson, behind the simple event, the one thing, is the vestigial serpent of Calvinist self-consciousness and introspection, of a kind with Emily Dickinson's. Divorced from specific dogma and particular religious zeal, it nonetheless continually circles around the problem of the nature of the universe. Frost may tell us in this regard that "the strong are saying nothing until they see," but we are not to assume that they never make judgments; in fact it sometimes seems that Frost implies a great deal, as Trilling observed, but that his characteristic metaphorical approach buries the meaning, so to speak, from the sight of those not ready to gaze unflinchingly. Such innocuous-seeming poems as "Spring Pools," "Once by the Pacific," "Fire and Ice," "Neither Out Far Nor In Deep," to name only a few of the better known, all imply the sense of possible disaster, of threat which Robinson too conveys sinisterly in "Luke Havergal," fatalistically yet with bitterness in "For a Dead Lady." It is no wonder that both poets took pains to hide their intent: there are some things not fitten for some people to know, as Frost once told an interviewer.

The religious sense, then, like a vestigial organ, remains, and unlike that organ has a true function in keeping the poet honest. He looks into his soul, not his id, with the intention of looking out again. The real world exists for him, sometimes triumphantly as is certainly the case with Cummings and only less so with Frost and Robinson because they are less the lyricists and more intellectual, if that is the appropriate word. Phelps Putnam, that lost soul, tried to make a pagan religion of his own with a do-it-yourself-kit assembled from various parts of youth and Yale and friends and sex. Fully aware that it did not, could not, work, he may perhaps have hoped that, like Yeats, he could simply make believe with it for the purpose of getting poems written. He could not be François Villon, try as he might; New England hardly deals in such products! But he could and did kill himself trying:

> And that is all I know about the flower;
> I have eaten it—it has disappeared.
> There is no Rose.

Whatever divinity one may torture out of sensuality, depravity, the "Closing and secret bud one might achieve / By
long debauchery"—whatever the true source of that new
religion which shall free men to be their true selves, it
is consumed in the ardor of pursuit. This particular theme
runs through much of Putnam's poetry, most strikingly in
what must be his finest poem, "Ballad of A Strange Thing."
Here in the pastoral New England of the fairly recent past
the poet evokes a pagan landscape, mood and tone, yet with
none of the elaborate rhetoric one might suppose necessary.
Greek myths (here, those of Apollo and Daphne and of
Pan) seem to spring naturally from the soil of this golden,
autumnal land, yet Putnam cannot really resolve the various elements of his feeling and thought—his pagan,
mythological hero, the Jack Chance of the poem, simply
goes away from the town of Pollard Mill, leaving everyone
"more / Dull and baffled than before."

The question we might ask here is: can these modern
New England poets see in the religious temper anything
more vital and lasting than on the one hand nostalgia; on
the other, the desire to find something—anything—that
will make them *feel*? In many of Putnam's poems, the
speaker laments the fact that he can no longer engage
naturally and spontaneously in sex, in love; even liquor
has lost its power and one needs more and more to achieve
ecstasy or the illusion of it. War, that other drug, has no
meaning and can no longer work. The characters in these
poems are in hell. Can we wonder that other poets since
Putnam have tried to map that hell, and to begin with, see
themselves as maimed Fausts: "Why this is hell nor am I
out of it." It is the hell of Robert Lowell's sanitarium where
the "Mayflower screwballs" go (at exorbitant rates) for safe-
keeping. And where do they go when they are "cured"?
back home where, as Lowell says: "Recuperating, I neither

spin nor toil." And it will go on like this forever, in this world and the next if there is one. The hell of self seems for Lowell and his school inescapable, final, complete, and by long experience, familiar, at last to be embraced. Lowell himself seems to cling, faintly, to the possibility of a kind of working salvation through the love of, or dependence upon, another, though he seems equally to imply that the other may be destroyed in the general desolation wrought by the "screwball" that is himself:

> your old-fashioned tirade—
> loving, rapid, merciless—
> breaks like the Atlantic Ocean on my head.

The indignant "another"—the wife—at the end of her tether gives the sufferer relief by acting like his ancestors who are, however seeming-cruel, loving and one's own. One can at least hate one's mother, and that is more than one can do for the bland professionals of the sanitarium. The poet comes to the conclusion that hell is where he is. He must learn to like it.

The chronology involved in this discussion seems to lead us surely enough to the conclusion that things get worse as they get older. That may in part be true; however, we must certainly agree that for all these poets hell is the self and the only redemption is by love. True, Anne Sexton and others make little if anything of the idea of redemption, and in her poems love is a kind of fitful easing of pain in temporary anesthesia. Yet there is self-love in the poems and from time to time a hesitant reaching out, as though to ask if another might be able to reach, too. Much of the problem in dealing with these poets, however, can be if not solved at least simplified if we look at the central issue as one of rhetoric. The modes and means of expression have changed since the days of Emerson and Dickinson and Robinson. We cannot look at nature as Frost did nor at personal relationships as Robinson did—not because they were wrong and we are right or the contrary, but simply because time has given us another angle of vision. In Robinson's poem "The Gift of God" we get an ironic, detached, yet sympathetic view of a woman whose love for her son is so strong that it can override the facts of the youth's real nature and abilities. The irony and detachment serve to distance the persons so that we shall not identify but see—and it may be, understand. Not so with Lowell, who wants us to feel the agony and self-contempt behind the word *screwball* as he applies it to himself. Contempt and agony, yes; but distance, no. We are to identify with the poet here and elsewhere, as Shelley wants his readers to when he bleeds, faints, fails. Frost will have none of this. The reticences in such a poetry as his and Robinson's seem faintly forbidding and hostile to many moderns, who would expect to be scolded and punished for delinquency and unbardlike activities were these ancestors alive and in a position to enforce their poetics as a legal system. Is there something didactic, a touch schoolmasterish, in the work of these earlier poets? Perhaps they threaten, cajole, actually punish—but is it not all done in love, that "old-fashioned tirade"?

Of course, love is a drug in the "litcrit" and pop markets these days; no poet or novelist can hope for any response unless he talks endlessly about it. But here we mean something like Christian or redemptive love, the kind that Cummings knows and can convey so simply when he hits it just right:

> My father moved through dooms of love
> through sames of am through haves of give
> singing each morning out of each night
> my father moved through depths of height

The spontaneous overflow of natural emotion, be it love or hate or anger or lust, is what Cummings calls life and what he celebrates. To the other poets considered here, such an overflow is impossible. There are degrees and degrees of self-consciousness and to Frost, for example, the

approach of Cummings is as impossible as it is to Lowell.
And there are many readers for whom Cummings's work
seems less childlike than childish, as of course it can be at
times. But the main point is that the poems frequently
show how hard won that direct, lyric simplicity was, how
the movement from destruction to celebration came as a
gradual and transforming spirit. Cummings repeats himself
almost endlessly, but the true theme is the celebration of
the incarnate. Though Frost may almost sourly say that
"One had to be versed in country things / Not to believe
the phoebes wept," we don't have to take Frost to mean
that a poetry like Cummings's is sentimental throughout.
Differences of temperament and of vision: these make art
rich. Robinson can show us a kind of love in "Eros Turannos" that makes us shudder, and in "Two Gardens in
Linndale" he gives us a love so wryly, sweetly transcendent
that it is a marvel that he stays clear of bathos, but he
triumphantly does. The two brothers of the poem, totally
independent yet totally involved in one another, show what
a kind of brotherly love and friendship and faith can mean.

The final word about love in this sense can never be
said. If many modern poets and novelists have lost the
power to celebrate and can only lament the loss, at least
some of them—Lowell might be one—seem to be looking
for various forms of love, almost as though they were
scientists in a laboratory. If love cannot be felt, they seem
to say, it can be investigated and ultimately, perhaps, rediscovered as feeling. The religious stages through which
some of these poets have passed come to look, to the reader,
like "a stairway to the sea / Where down the blind are
driven." The self-consciousness and self-analysis that many
contemporaries give us in their verse seem at last both
compulsive and escapist—romanticism in its ultimate form.
The "only connect" that E. M. Forster demanded of all
men seems an impossibility—for the present at any rate.
These poets are frequently like the lobotomized Lepke in
Lowell's "Memories of West Street and Lepke": "hanging

like an oasis in his air / of lost connections"; or, in "Skunk Hour," "I myself am hell; / nobody's here." Does the great gulf between Robinson, Frost, Cummings, and the contemporary school simply symbolize the change in the times? Does the scrapping of his Roman Catholic faith on Lowell's part signify that orthodoxy of any kind is finished and we are a society of free lances? Surely since Blake poets have been heterodox for the most part, when not atheist or indifferent, but most would say with Conrad's old Garibaldino in *Nostromo*, "God is for men; religion is for women." Frost tells us, "Earth's the right place for love; I don't know where / It's likely to go better," and Robinson, in "The Three Taverns," "I that have lost all else / For wisdom and the wealth of it, say now / To you that out of wisdom has come love." For both poets, love seems to be something that is neither earned nor deserved but given. It simply happens. For Cummings it is the condition of life: "Love is the whole and more than all"; for Phelps Putnam it is the "melting lie." For all these poets as for all the rest of us, it remains a matter of belief and definition; in a word, the Word—made flesh and dwelling among us. Lowell, "gored by the climacteric of his want" shows love in extremis—solipsistic, agonized, bloody. The function of criticism at the present time, to go back to Arnold, may only be to say again that we have split the word and the thing, the emotion and the response, so far apart that love means nothing at all. How can it mean when it cannot be? If Putnam calls it a lie, Hart Crane goes one better: "Lie to us! Dance us back our tribal morn." Love then is illusion. Wholly without faith, we may make it up again as metaphor: not less, but more, than all. Obscurantist perhaps? Yes—but a way to get poems written. In that sense, belief and religion are what can be made to work.

History and Imagination

Once upon a time a man wrote a book with the catchy title *The World as Will and Idea*. Today a philosopher might more appropriately call his grand synthesis or disaster *The World as Analogy*. It does seem that sociologists, media men, pop psychologists, dropped-out presidential aides, and turned-on clerics go in heavily for making the world out to be some kind of analogical picture of their own uneases or fixed ideas. Some years ago Einsteinian analogies were In: the space-time continuum was the magic phrase. But we've changed all that. Now it is either, on the hip hand All-New Spaceship Earth, Buckminster Fuller via Jules Verne, or on the other or square hand, it is Structuralism, Structural Linguistics, Structural Anthropology and if we don't watch out, Structural History and Structural you and me. The name to conjure with is not Einstein—not even Marcuse or Frantz Fanon or Che or Mao—but Claude Lévi-Straus, the guru who inherits Einstein's mantle because everyone invokes him and no one understands him. But he should not be understood—merely invoked, like God.

History as Structuralism we shall have to consider, God help us. At the moment, though, let us, or rather me, give vent to some old-fashioned ideas about history and I'll start with this one: History as Continuum.

Without a sense of the past, we live, not in the present, but in a future that does not, can not, happen. Past, present, and future make a continuum in time and space, so that if one denies the present in favor of a more rewarding past, one removes the possibility of going anywhere; one denies where one should go and hence falsifies where one came from. On the other hand, if a man denies his past in favor of a total present, he prohibits the future, since the future is merely an imaginary state of becoming and as such constantly becomes the present and then the past. The past existed—that we know because we are here and came from somewhere. But we do not know where we are going nor indeed if going we are. We know only that when we actually do go somewhere it is not into the future, only another present. In order then to believe that the world is anything other than a huge, indifferent, and undifferentiated now, we must believe in Before and After. Nearly all the willed ignorance and obscurantism of our age and others comes as a result of denial. We deny our past and others' pasts. It is only recently, I think, that we in this country have begun to realize just how much we have denied ourselves and others.

I hope to touch, as briefly and as clearly as my slender understanding will permit, on this matter of structuralism and the imaginative use of the past as I go along; not systematically, but not too impressionistically either, whatever that *too* may mean.

What is history? Obviously, this is a question no one can answer though a great many try. The point might better be, why ask such a question? But then, questions are what's happening these days and answers seem in short supply when they are not merely outrageous. A few years ago E. H. Carr of Trinity, Cambridge, gave as his Trevelyan lectures a series entitled "What is History," the best part of which was the epigraph to the published version, a quotation from Jane Austen's *Northanger Abbey*: "I often think it odd that it should be so dull for a great deal of it must be invention." Jane Austen's wit says succinctly what Professor Carr never quite says at all: namely, that history is what historians make it, history with a capital H, that is. To the layman, it is "he who died o' Wednesday," what did happen back then and is all over with, we hope. To the unsophisticated man or woman who is curious about the past and wants to know about it, history is people and large events, doings, grand passions, or perhaps artifacts and flowers.

Well now, what does the new breed of historian have

to say? What questions does he ask of the past and of past histories of the past? He comes with a powerful armament of new and subversive notions about what history and historians do or should do. Like his fellow political liberals or radicals, he finds that most former writers of history have been blind to the real issues, which are in his view chiefly these two: first, that history has until the present time ignored race, subcultures, and the historical underground in favor of aristocracy, economics, and power politics, and second, that it is not so much a question of what history is or was as it is one of what history is for, its use and true purpose. And here we have a truly subversive idea, I think, one that may be of great liberating value while at the same time it can be used to propagandistic ends. But after all, the only thing more tendentious than history written by an individual with all of an individual's personal limitations, prejudices, and ignorance is history written as it were by the hand of God or of a committee, all fake objectivity and pseudofacts.

The contemporary radical historian is a revisionist and a reformer, indeed almost a historical anarchist. Taking his cue in part at least from Claude Lévi-Straus, he attempts a structuralist version of history in which all parts of the social milieu of a particular era form a kind of grammar for that language which is the history of that time. If one single element of that complex grammar is slighted or left out, the language falls silent, tells lies or stammers. History, then, in the view of the modernist, has its true function in its capturing of the social dynamics of a particular racial, ethnic, social minority. Show me, the historian says, how a minority fares in a society and I will tell you what that society is up to. It is usually, of course, up to no good. But the historian wants to emphasize the enormous gap between what a society thinks it is doing and what it really does; what it fancies its aims to be and what it really brings about. The disparity between these two constitutes the field of error in which former histories have gone astray.

Our modern historian wants to narrow the gap, to bridge it, fill it. He wants to make history into an instrument of reform, of revolution. History will make us see the real truth about ourselves and our society and make us want to begin again on a different basis. Know the truth and the truth shall make you free.

Maybe we wish it were like that. Unfortunately, most of us, confronted with the spectacle of man's inhumanity to man, are more likely to think, Know the truth and the truth shall make you sick. We might even go back to and along with Henry Ford and say, history is bunk. Or that what we learn from history is that we do not learn from history. Or maybe just learn to avoid it. But the sad part is, it won't go away. As Robert Penn Warren says: "The world is real, it is there." Of course it is. But is it? The subtle power of Warren's statement—mostly derived from what comes before in the poem—lies in its complex irony. Dr. Johnson kicking the stone, Pangloss contracting venereal disease, Socrates dying the death: what do these things mean if not that all human life is composed of an elaborate series of maneuvers on the part of us all to avoid the realization that "most things break," as Robinson's Eben Flood puts it. All the philosophy in the world and out of it can't help. History may console. Misery loves company. To read about our Civil War is a livelier read than the Critique of Pure Reason. But is it truer? Warren would assert that nothing is real or true until it has been proved in the blood and on the nerves and in the heart. If the world is an illusion, we who feel it, nonetheless, must act as though it had shape, texture, and presence. We have broken ourselves against it and we know.

The point is, though, we don't know much and that little too late. And another point should be, I think, that history is after all a metaphor. We imagine the past; we cannot know it because we do not live there. All is illusion and what counts is to make the illusion correspond as fully to an imagined reality as the human imagination can contrive. Aristotle was not fooling when he claimed that poetry was superior to history. Poetry, like myth, may help us to be, to live. Lévi-Strauss claims that all myths have as their true function the individual's better accommodation to the world of his daily living. *We* have no "real" myths. Mythologized history is merely lies, but real myth is like metaphor: we act "as if," we call one thing by the name of another, we look at reality askance, like the lookout who knows that what one stares at goes invisible, that one sees the real in a casual glance.

All of which brings us back to Catherine Moreland of *Northanger Abbey* and her all-unknowing profundity: "I often think it odd that it [history] should be so dull for a great deal of it must be invention." Much is, but then neither the historian nor the reader knows that it is in any given instance, both being well deceived. But the poet "never lieth," as Sir Philip Sidney says, "for he nothing affirmeth." In other words, the poet, the inventor and the contriver of imaginary events and people, does not claim that his world is true, only that it is real, exemplary, a metaphor. Horace wrote that there were great men before Agamemnon, but they had no bards, no Homer, to make them real, to commend them fully and unforgettably to the imagination. Why do so many black writers and intellectuals of today complain that they have been robbed of their past? Because without a sense of one's past as person and as part of a world or society or race or nation, one has no identity. When we robbed the black man of his history, we in a real sense robbed him of his soul. Black writers today search for that soul, and find it, in poems, plays, and novels. Up till now they had only their music, and we are trying to take that away from them, have indeed done so in part; but as they more and more discover their past, recreate and imagine it in literature, they pass by much of a white world that lives on cheap fancies and commercials and tries to forget the dire prophecies of the future.

But now I want to turn to the exemplary material of

my own experience. Many writers use and abuse history
for their own purposes, and it's no use blaming poetry for
bad plays and poems and poets. What I should like to do
here is to get down to a particular case: my own attempt to
write a play for the sesquicentennial of the state of Maine.

All of us, when we think about history at all, tend to
think of it as something that happened—that *was*. We take
note of an event in our own time and ask how it will be
treated in "the history books," the implication being that
that is where history goes to die! In other words, history
tells how things were, and anything else is not "true." An
old Greek named Aristotle said that poetry was superior
to history because it was more philosophical, and he may
have been right; but most of us, when we read a poem or
see a play based upon "real"—as opposed to fictitious—
events and persons, expect to be lied to about what actually
happened, forgetting that facts are notorious liars particularly when they pretend to truth, whereas a valid play
or poem or novel aims at telling us not how things *were*,
but how they *felt*—how they felt and smelled and tasted
and looked. And that requires an effort of the imagination.

I have been perplexed by the comment many people
have made to me in connection with the play *Birth of a
State*, that it seems so "contemporary"—as though that
were not only remarkable but a good thing! I don't quite
see it that way. The events had their remarkable qualities,
true enough, but what struck me was the uniqueness or
salty quality of the men involved—some of them, at any
rate. William King, Maine's first governor, was a remarkable
man who knew what he wanted for Maine and for himself.
Uneducated, yet with two half brothers who had gone to
Harvard, he had many personal and other reasons for wanting to outdo others, yet joined with such a motive one finds
all kinds of complications, plain to see in the "history books"
and requiring only putting oneself in the place of King to
imagine. Similarly, his colleague John Holmes, the man
who went to Washington to head the drive to push state-

hood through the Congress, appeals equally strongly to the imagination. Sensitive, slightly withdrawn, reflective, Holmes seems an odd, yet really inevitable, counterpart to King. Could a playwright find a better dramatic point of departure? Then couple those two with one or two representative figures of the age and the circumstances and you have it all there. Now you just have to write it!

History helped here. Maine had gone through some hard and nearly catastrophic times; the War of 1812 had ravaged much of the coast, and nobody but Maine folk cared. Massachusetts, to which Maine belonged, was untouched yet seemed to want King, then general of the militia, to send troops to protect Boston! And then there were hard times after the war—trade embargoes, emigration, crop failures—all the usual afflictions of an isolated and dependent community or country. Poverty and hardship were widespread, and the gap between rich and poor was great and growing. In these circumstances a group of men met to work out a constitution for a new state that should cut loose from old ties and make a new start. Did they know what they were up to? The historian tries to find the document that will say yes or no; the historical imagination looks at King and Holmes and thinks, "Yes *and* No."

Men do not feel their motives as single and pure. Motives come in all sorts of adulterated mixtures and William King was not so extraordinary that he felt motives pure. But the point is that for drama to emerge from these matters, there must be a lively setting forth of people's motives and feelings in action. Most people act in two ways—by what they do and by what they say, and drama is made up of both. The men, or many of them, who composed Maine's constitutional convention were good talkers and good thinkers. The words and ideas and opinions that lie buried in the record come alive when one touches them with the imagination. The contemporary quality that many seemed to find in the play derives less from the specific issues involved than from the persons who fought for or against

issues, ideas, prejudices. The drama is in the men and their
views, and how they came to hold those views, just as much
as it lies in mere questions of how to settle the matter of
suffrage or of legislative representation. Facts are inert until
we feel them.

It is for example a fact that Maine achieved statehood
because of the Missouri Compromise. Massachusetts had
set a deadline for the adoption of a constitution and the
passage of Maine's petition through Congress. It seemed
perhaps more than fact warranted that haste or at least
dispatch was required, and Holmes, along with others,
knew that. Hence, Maine bought its statehood at the price
of supporting the Missouri Compromise. And there are
historians who, if they know nothing else of Maine, know
that fact. Yet what does that fact mean in isolation? Maine
held no brief for slavery, nor did she feel that black men
were inferior to white. Indeed, the history of Maine from
1820 through the Civil War shows that most of the population wanted freedom for all men and did something about
it. Nevertheless, constitutions and governments are made
by, even if sometimes they don't seem to be made for, men.
Men like William King are interesting above all because they
combine in their natures the utterly pragmatic and the
idealistic, the self-serving and the selfless. It is no wonder
a man so thoughtful, wise, and inward as Holmes should
fall under the influence of King, and King under his—a
curious partnership but one not at all uncommon when both
parties have the gift of imagination. They feel what it might
be like to have in their own natures the qualities of the
other man's. Hamlet and Horatio. Wellington and Nelson.
Acheson and Truman. One could go on indefinitely. But
it becomes apparent in all such cases that the men themselves think of themselves dramatically, as caught up in
affairs that have the elements of human and historical drama. And they enjoy the game. The quality of zest and spirit
not only gives the events the flavor they retain long after any
urgency has departed, but that quality seems to speak

strongly to the imaginative reader or observer—speaks most
strongly of all—even today and even in a time when we are
usually told that men have very little effect on their time;
it is only "forces" and "movements." Whenever we come
across a historical figure, great or small, who brings to
events, great or small, a communicated sense of excitement,
zest, and brilliance—why then we remember and celebrate
the man and the affair, since he is the one who made the
matter dramatic, made it "true," if you like.

Governor King went almost from rags to riches and
back again. He could love and hate and be loved and hated
in return. Although he aspired to leadership—could and
did, in fact, lead—he was no politician. Hard to imagine him
courting the voters and keeping his mouth shut for fear
of losing elections! The achieving of statehood for Maine
was for him an aim which, if not absolutely final, was certainly a chief goal. He set about getting that constitution
single-mindedly; and if I am any judge, he set about making
himself Maine's first governor with equal determination.
Not because he was all that ambitious politically but because
(as I think) he wanted to show those fancy Harvard brothers
of his who was really the prize of the family—and also to
bind together for all time the names of Maine and King.
And of course his follower, his counselor and sometimes
better nature, Holmes, knew those things very well and did
not love the man less for them. In King they did not appear
petty or mean or deceitful; they seemed almost endearing.
And since Holmes, like most sensitive and imaginative
souls, recognized that in King's friendship for him there
was an element of condescension—for the impractical
dreamer, you might say—he also, humanly, could patronize
King in turn for his human foibles. The drama of the men
would seem to be clear, yet how does one find drama in a
convention—unless it's in the smoke-filled rooms of legend?

I suppose the answer has to be the truism that drama
is conflict, and there was plenty of that. Towns versus
country, the farmer versus the merchant, Federalist versus

Jacksonian democrat—all kinds of conflicts and passionate disagreement. Yet here again, it is the men that drama arises from. King was a thoroughgoing democrat of the Jacksonian sort—with a kind of highhandedness too that lots of democrats can display without sensing any inconsistency. King had little affection for the aristocratic Federalists, who of course would have made fun of his crude vocabulary and bad grammar. But he was no antiintellectual know-nothing. He did not flatter ignorance nor seek to make his own lack of education a goal for others to strive for. He knew his own limitations, but he also had the humility and intelligence to seek out men like Holmes who could make up for his own deficiencies with their brains and education and trained insight. As a result, for the dramatist trying to find a way to get hold of the essence of the drama in the constitutional convention, the solution finally seemed to lie in pitting man against man and bringing them together at the end—along with the ideas and aims they fought for or against.

Much depends on the individual playwright's own nature and hence his reading of the facts of history as to whether his ending will be "happy" or unhappy; if he is commissioned to celebrate an aspect of the state of Maine's sesquicentennial, he can't really expect to take dim views or view with alarm. But perhaps he can ask Maine men and women of today to look back at their forebears and compare them with the gentlemen in Augusta and in Washington and make a few deductions. History is to blame, not the dramatist, if we find that perhaps today's crop doesn't bear comparison very well. But the playwright also hopes that the Maine man or woman of today will ask if perhaps it's a combination of the man and the moment that make for "greatness." William King was not a Great Man but he could rise to certain occasions greatly. He was a "man of the people" too, and I suppose that a true democrat believes that the true man of the people must be one who can and does rise to great occasions with greatness. The play

Birth of a State attempts to show William King exemplifying these democratic qualities. And I should perhaps also explain that I don't necessarily assert that that's how it was, or how it will be, but one often has to act as though something were "true" which isn't!

Finally, I should affirm my belief that history has no purpose as a study or subject of discourse if it does not stir and awaken people. In our own time we see and hear much that makes history into a kind of superpatriotic spectacular on the one hand, or on the other hand a set of lies that we must rigorously expose. Both such views corrupt us, but even more they deprive us of the possibility of meaning. The men who framed Maine's constitution, like all men, served false gods as well as true. Does that mean that only the false gods exist, or that there are no gods at all? What it really means, I think, is that men are not gods but that at times, under certain conditions, men like King and Holmes and others can rise to that degree of greatness possible to them—or in rare cases, higher. Just as they can sink below it. Maybe that isn't history—most historians would say it isn't—but it is poetry. Which is better. Didn't Aristotle say so? As though we didn't know it anyhow.

You Never Can Tell:
George Bernard Shaw Reviewed

Writers and artists generally must be in love with reality. Humanity, higher in the scale than animals and therefore incapable of total unself-consciousness, must strive for that totality of experience that only complete self-consciousness can give. For the stuff of life is action and experience, as it is of art, yet by means of art alone can we participate fully and with absolute awareness the very while we are experiencing. Obviously those who experience nothing or derive nothing from experience have little notion of reality, for true reality is the experience of it—nothing less—and hence the writer, if he is to be called great (whatever that means) must be in love with reality, must provide for us as readers an experience of reality that brings into play all the resources of mind, sense, and spirit.

The art closest to the actual world of people, things, and experience is, of course, the drama. If drama is not active, direct and empirical, it is nothing, and the dramatist who has no direct contact with a stage, actors and the problems they involve creates no dramas. I do not mean by this, as I shall make plain, that naturalism or realism forms the basis of every successful play, though in a sense I do mean exactly that; what is crucial here is that we realize how close drama must be to life, which is of course why it so often dates hopelessly. Where, for example, is Sir Arthur Wing Pinero, William Archer's candidate for immortality? How many of us would rapturously hail a revival of Dion Boucicault's *London Assurance,* of Barrie's *The Admirable Crichton*, of Clifford Odets's *Waiting for Lefty*? They mirrored their times, certainly, but, the substance gone, can the image of it remain? Yet when the drama does not date, when the substance of the time is imperishable and the image of it both just and profound, as in Etherege's *The Man of*

Mode or in Sean O'Casey's *The Plough and the Stars*, how vital and potent above the other literary forms it seems to most of us—how robust, crowded, and above all things, conscious.

It is this extension of consciousness that the greatest dramatists and writers in general strive to effect, and in many cases their efforts to this end concern themselves with the eternal problem of appearance and reality, most particularly manifested in the exposure of humbug, deceit, and hypocrisy, wherever found. And the good dramatist finds them everywhere. Why not? The discrepancy between seeming and being, between the ideal and the actual, finds constant expression in most good work (and much bad): in *Measure for Measure*, in just about all poetry, in Conrad's *Nostromo*, in James Gould Cozzens's *Guard of Honor*, as well as in the works of Truman Capote and Mickey Spillane. If this is to imply that the great artists are preeminently great moralists, such implication is scarcely unprecedented; it is precisely because the dramatist *shows* morals and mores in action that he is so potent a force for good or evil in the moral realm. One need only read, or better, see a play or two by Shakespeare, Ben Jonson, Wycherly, Congreve to find the line that leads to Shaw. As Shaw himself says, he stands on Shakespeare's shoulders, though many of us would perhaps see a closer tie with other more nearly contemporary playwrights. Too often we look at the work of men like Congreve and the Restoration dramatists in general, to give only one example, as either a pernicious mirroring of a licentious age or else as an amoral fantasy conjured up from a never-never land where all men are handsome and all the girls are game. Similarly, we have a tendency to think of Shaw as that rapidly obsolescing radical or as old George Bernard Shaw the prankster and buffoon. Why is it that these illusions arise and perpetuate themselves? Why do we continue, when the plays are before us, to enjoy the entertainment without ever giving to the play itself that tribute of total consciousness both a Congreve and a Shaw demand? Why will we not take them seriously?

Obviously, because we like to keep things simple. We want the direct approach of solemnity or of yaks and boffs or of sentimental empathy unalloyed. This the best playwrights will not allow. In *The Way of the World*, for example, Congreve forbids us the easy way of identification with hero or heroine while we hiss the villain and weep for his wicked deeds: the elements of good and evil are mingled; thus the hypocrite Fainall at first seems to us the man of true wit, as Witwoud seems the delightful humorist, the real card. Only gradually do we begin to see how man's ego has worked in these folk with pride to warp nature, to give to each character certain affected airs, so that in the end we observe that only Millamant and Mirabell have been able to preserve integrity and spirit and essential grace despite the corrupting influence of the world. Despite? No, perhaps indeed *because* of the world. For in their delicate maneuvering whereby they come close to destruction yet always beautifully escape lies the fascination of the play and Congreve's morality and aesthetic. No morality and no art without risks; that seems to be much of the point. Millamant and Mirabell go their way and achieve and deserve one another because of their fine sense that life consists in taking chances and in outmaneuvering the world while they flirt with it. A dangerous game, yet how exciting and stimulating—how wholly conscious, not for children or the naive. With open eyes and minds these folk accept the facts of existence without cynicism or gullibility; they accept but do not truckle. Their very acceptance, the while they remain essentially uninvolved, represents their triumph and Congreve's, artistically and morally.

All this is in the tradition. This is Prospero in *The Tempest*. From another aspect, we see the same concern in Jonson's *Volpone* and Wycherly's *The Country Wife*. In the latter play one is struck by the repetition of the word "affectation"; the characters affect a wit or a sense of honor or virtue they do not have. Horner, the terror of husbands, affects impotence in order to cuckold husbands. The world corrupts those who have neither the inherent grace nor the acquired character to outmaneuver or resist. So with Jonson, in *Volpone*, the world comes before us as lust, naked and brutal, debasing and deforming at large. And all the characters of these playwrights, Jonson's, Congreve's, Wycherly's, when they suffer defeat, do so as the victims of their own self-deception, their affectations, their false humors, their lusts.

And lust is manifold. Sexuality is the commonest device the drama has known; yet Jonson gives us others: lust for power and riches, for reputation or for notoriety. Congreve shows us similar aspects of lust in Witwoud, Fainall, and Lady Wishfort. Always the root of lust is self-deception and its fruit depravity. Above all, these playwrights see that behind the desire to deceive and be deceived lies the urge to avoid reality, to turn the self into something it can not in nature be, and always the result is ruin and chaos. The tradition is as old as great art itself, and Shaw belongs very clearly at the center of it. Has he not told us how he cribbed his plots from anywhere and borrowed wholesale from Dickens? More than this, however, he has taken his morality direct from the masters of drama in the English tradition. His philosophy, of course, his social and political beliefs are easy to trace, since Shaw himself spreads the record before us in the prefaces and in such abstract documentaries as his *Back to Methuselah* cycle. Clearly, Bergson and Nietzsche and William Blake have had a hand in the forming of Shaw's mind and purpose: Bergson's élan vital is Shaw's Creative Evolution, the doctrine of spiritual growth which Shaw considers the new religion. John Tanner's "Revolutionist's Handbook" in *Man and Superman* recalls Blake's "Proverbs of Hell" as the play itself reminds of Nietzsche. Few playwrights have had the knowledge and sense of the past that Shaw had, nor can we imagine social and moral criticism of any real cogency that has no basis in an acute sense of history. The prologue to *Caesar and Cleopatra* alone makes this clear: our business is with the present and future, yet there can be neither awareness nor intelligence of them if we will not consider and try to cope with our history. Only in such an effort can we live, become part of the life force, become capable of metaphysical truth. Knowledge of the self and of the world of the self: these we must have if the life force is not to pass us by and evolve another species. We can no longer be content to "banish mind from the universe," to use the phrase of Samuel Butler's that Shaw was so fond of quoting.

Well, you can corner me smartly enough now and anticipate my conclusion: great books must be in the tradition and particularly in the tradition of morality that has informed drama from early times. Most Shavians are aware of Shaw's strictures on Shakespeare and of his apparently absurd comparisons of himself with the great bard, yet when Shaw comes down to Shakespeare one sees what he means well enough: he means that bardolatry and Shakespeare are two quite different things; that Shaw loves the Shakespeare who is the master of reality.

The correspondence is easier to hit on than one might suppose. Each refuses to fall slave to opinions and abstract ideas, refuses to become "a pet lamb in a sentimental farce." To the best poets and dramatists, full-blooded life provides the moral, the problem, and the solution. John Tanner, Joan, Caesar—call the roll of the Shavian heroes and heroines, those folk who possess "the evolutionary appetite," who are wholly caught up in the life force: all know this élan vital, this love affair with reality. Appearance and reality, seeming and being. Is not that the key to much of Shakespeare? To *Hamlet* and *Troilus and Cressida* and *Measure for Measure*? In the latter play, the Duke would know "what our seemers be," as Hamlet, rejecting Horatio's rebuke that " 'Twere to consider too curiously to consider so" replies, "No, faith, not a jot." You remember the scene—by Ophelia's grave, Hamlet holding the skull of Yorick, the reality, and saying, "Get you to my lady's chamber and tell her, let her paint an inch thick, to this favor she must come." And then speculating that the dust of Alexander might stop up a bunghole. We call this morbid, perhaps, yet it is of a piece with that vision of reality reduced to its constituents which we find in Jonson's comedies, in the fierce sexualities of Wycherly, in the naked vision of human motives and self-deception expressed in John de Stogumber's cruelty in *Saint Joan*. Throughout Shaw's plays we feel constantly the pressure of reality on illusion, whether it take comic form in the silly, romantic notions turned topsy-turvy in *Arms and the Man* or near-tragic scope in the exploding of self-deception in *Heartbreak House*. Shaw lusts to know and to show what our seemers be, and he will consider as curiously as he in nature can to find out, and then to dramatize what he finds.

II

What is new about this? Why seems it so particular with Shaw? Shaw knows not Seems; he makes the very tissue and texture of his work of that material we find throughout the best English drama—Shakespeare, Ben Jonson, Congreve, Wycherly. Yet clearly Shaw's genius is more allied to that of Congreve or of Jonson—or in his own view that of Molière; for Shaw is an abstract thinker as well as an artist, and the rationale of his work is propaganda of one sort or another. And here we could add that the prototype of Shaw, more than any of the playwrights mentioned, might well be Dickens, whom Shaw admired and copied. Propaganda, caricature, excess, epic sweep—we associate these qualities with Dickens and we can easily do the same with Shaw provided we understand that he controls his art better and has the more perfect sense of reality. Yet the basis of the resemblance goes deep, even to the profound source of energy in all literature, namely motion. The drama has as its purpose, revelation; as its vehicle, motion; and of the motions possible to it speech is the most important, a fact that present-day playwrights seem to have forgotten if they ever knew it. As in Dickens's novels, motion in Shaw's plays is outward, is centrifugal rather than centripetal, moving outward to a circumference of meaning which though finite is unbounded. The idea is the igniter, lighting off the boilers that create the head of steam—the power and movement of the play. So of course Shaw puts the central meanings, the essential didacticism, in the prefaces and then sets his play in motion with the propagandist idea, driving it toward the circumference. He knows perfectly well that he can attract into his orbit only those people who enjoy life; equally he knows that to attract them he must *make* them enjoy aspects of life not commonly associated with enjoyment. Hence Shaw the buffoon in the popular press, Shaw the writer of successful movie scenarios. And he knocks us out, with his Enery Igginses and Snobby Prices, as Dickens does with his Sam Wellers and Reverend Chadbands. Oh, yes, they are both a couple of cards.

Well, how about this motion in drama? We see clearly what it is in Congreve, say, in *The Way of the World*, where all the movement glides in and out, brings characters together, separates them, holds the group in delicate equipoise a moment, then scatters it to prepare for a new combining. So it is with Molière in *The Misanthrope*. And Shaw can better such instruction. Notice, how, in *You Never Can Tell*, people move on and off stage, combine, move away, reform. Consider the final scene, for example, in which attention shifts from a single character to a group, while people move on and off—Bohun, Walter, Dolly, and Phil. Or, the luncheon scene, the ballet of waiters. Plenty of movement. Yet essentially—and those who have seen the recent production of *Don Juan in Hell* will be well aware of this—the motion arises from talk, from language as action, from the interplay of idea with expression, from the reversals and combining of speech. And always in a situation; always with

an eye to the one speaking, the ones spoken to, and the general temper of the moment. And such a prose—easy, virile,
economical, speech recognizably speakable—yet how much
we wish we could speak like that! For the duration of the
play, we do indeed speak like that; we become for the moment the completely aware creatures Shaw demands that we
become, using our full capacity for enjoyment, understanding, criticism, while we experience to the full. How far this
is from the moving picture, the soap opera, the drama of
Tennessee Williams, the one demand of which is that we
abandon entirely any cerebration and simply turn ourselves
into the particular hero or heroine. No, Shaw will have none
of that. He positively forces us to remain ourselves while
he elevates those selves and pushes us out of familiar responses and patterns of experience into new environments
where the only familiar landmarks are the forms of Shaw's
own art.

The movement is centrifugal. It starts outside the plays
themselves with the prefaces and goes beyond the con-
ceptual or didactic in the dramaturgy itself. Like Jonson, like
Congreve, like Dickens, Shaw starts with a set of ideas or,
purportedly, a specific social question, and then uses this
as a symbol that ramifies as the play gathers force. So it
is with his characters: they move from the specific type to
the general human being, become as it were moral images
of human nature under certain stresses. Thus Crampton, in
You Never Can Tell, moves from a caricature of the sour
old puritan to a witty image of the unlovely person needing
love; "William" the Waiter from the typical Jeeves-of-all-
work to the perfect symbol of social ease and adjustment;
Gloria from the type of the strong-minded beauty to a perfect image of young womanhood suddenly shown her essential vulnerability and instinctual nature. And of course
the play seems like a bowling alley during a hard evening—
all those pins eternally being set up and as surely knocked
down again, as though the whole drama were a trope for
life itself. How Shaw refined this method the inveterate

Shavian knows; how in *Heartbreak House* the image is one
of sheer destruction, of stripping bare. Every single blessed
soul is stripped as naked as a jaybird and must recognize
its own awkward bare humanity. We must go a long way
from teasing comic reversal to serious stripping, yet the
motion in both cases is the same: from illusion to reality,
from the center outward, from the particular to the general. Yet Shaw does not avoid the center. He knows, to
use Eliot's verse, that "there the dance is, at the still point
of the turning world." The moral images, the circumambient
trope, must preserve reality in the situation, in the temper
of the scene, and in the specific nature of the moral problem
that arises from the social one.

Yet such comment might indicate that Shaw is a kind
of Ibsen with an English or a Dublin accent. What about
the humor, the farcical element, the sheer theatrical corn
so basic to Shaw's work? We are told too often that this
is just the old maestro sugaring the pill of doctrine and
didacticism—throwing a fish to the animals so that they
will swallow the cerebral sauce. Nonsense. Anybody who
has a reasonably adult acquaintance with the theater knows
that while this is a common theory it has one severe draw-
back: it doesn't work. You simply cannot mix genres in the
drama and expect an unmixed success. I refer any doubters
to the modern musical comedy (*sic*) where we find pathos,
farce, song-and-dance, arty ballet and sermon all together
in a mishmash pleasing to the tired executive but almost
unbearably irritating to the adult. What is vital here is
the question of tone on the one hand, and on the other that
of the artist's essential seriousness; in fine, whether or not
he has a genuine subject.

In Shaw's more imposing plays one thing emerges from
the start: a sense of locale, of time, period, and overriding
theme. We must in the very first few lines of the play know
precisely where we are, and in *Caesar and Cleopatra*, in
Heartbreak House, in *John Bull's Other Island* we are confronted with a dramatized image, within the first scene, of

the entire play and its significance. The fact that this may be done facetiously need not deter the serious spectator. Observe chiefly that Shaw can within such a scene sketch lightly for us the motifs to be developed, observe that a humorous beginning allows him the opportunity to use humor throughout the play without violating our sense of decorum. In other words, humor is to be of the very fabric of the action and movement. So *Saint Joan* begins with the absurd business about the hens not laying eggs and ends with them laying like mad. How silly, when you come right down to it— and how right. Again, how like Shaw to start a play in a dentist's office as he does in *You Never Can Tell.* Yet the scene not only gives us routine information but sets the tone: we have come here to have this nagging ache out, and if laughing gas will do it best, that's fine. *But*—extraction is the business in hand and we had better not forget it. Toothache is the human condition; as Bohun puts it, "It's unwise to be born; it's unwise to be married; it's unwise to live; and it's wise to die." The reality of the human condition is not changed by our private views of it. The masters of reality, the cosmic dentists, of Shaw's drama are forever begging us to have it out, now once and for all. You can go along for your normal span with a nagging toothache and it will only spoil your life and ruin you for any useful activity. Or you can have it out the hard way as Crampton demands, with no gas simply because you think unnecessary pain is good for sinful humans, as though there weren't enough pain of the inevitable sort. Or, like the masters of reality, you can pay a little extra, have it out and go on from there without fear, trauma, or hatred. Valentine is the actual dentist; Bohun is the spiritual dentist, and both throw reality in the swollen faces of the other characters. Have it out, they say: it may hurt a bit but not anywhere nearly as much as you think—certainly not as much as living with the rotting tooth in your jaw. Face up to what you are and what your essential needs are. Only by so doing can you put behind you all the folly and hurt of living a lie. Be a man, or a woman as the case may be, and be yourself—not what some unreal code tells you you should be.

And so the movement of Shaw's plays establishes its center in concrete instance, usually a kind of trope or image figuring forth the significance of the whole work, and then moves out to impinge upon a whole circumference of ideas and moral images related to but not confined by plot, action, and setting. The humor, both verbal and theatrical, has already set the tone and made it supple enough to allow many modulations. *Saint Joan* opens in the manner we remarked, yet by the purity of diction and the overtones of spiritual concern emerging from this absurd scene, Shaw is enabled to adumbrate the seriousness of his theme. The language has such economy and precision that it can within itself move us to grave attention and to laughter without any elaborate preparations for a new key: the possibilities of such change exist within the idiom itself. For example, look at the end of *Saint Joan*, scene one, and then at the opening of scene three—humor and grave meaning, seriousness and a light touch as well as a touch of poetic power that never for an instant slops over. I ask the curious to compare the language here with any to be found anywhere in Arthur Miller, Eugene O'Neill, Tennessee Williams—and yes indeed, Christopher Fry. Of T. S. Eliot we will not speak.

The point needs no great urging. Shaw simply writes the best dramatic language since Congreve; one might say the only dramatic language since Congreve. And this is almost enough for fine drama if into the bargain the dramatist have a genuine subject, though indeed I hold it an impossibility for a writer to write well about little or nothing. Yet as a corollary to this I would revert for a moment to the question of what I have been calling moral images and what that means specifically for character in drama, Shavian or other. And a brief glance at Shaw's own stage directions will bear me out, I think, in the contention that for him as for most good playwrights there is no such thing as a living character. There is instead only movement, the moral rhythm of a certain sort of person in a certain sort of situation. This is as far from living people as one can get: people we know and like do not often figure to us as types or standing for something, yet it is precisely this that they must do in a play. Here is a character in a Shaw play going through the paces Shaw marks off for him:

> Walpole returns with the newspaper man, a cheerful, affable young man who is disabled for ordinary business by a congenital erroneousness which renders him incapable of describing accurately anything he sees, or understanding or reporting accurately anything he hears. As the only employment in which these defects do not matter is journalism (for a newspaper, not having to act on its descriptions and reports but only to sell them to idly curious people has nothing but honor to lose by inaccuracy and unveracity), he has perforce become a journalist and has to keep up an air of high spirits through a daily struggle with his own illiteracy and the precariousness of his employment.

Now this is meant to be read, not acted, yet the journalist goes on to quote chapter and verse in his words and actions. All Shaw's characters do so, though they do not rest there. What is of major importance is that we observe how closely akin this attitude toward character is to that of Ben Jonson, to the comedy of Humors. These people represent something: they are embodiments of the feelings of a whole class. To that end Shaw does not try to make his characters interesting because of their plight or their emotional states; he rather makes interesting what they say and do and stand for and thus absorbs us not in empathetic self-pity but in critical appraisal and awareness. This is not to suggest that he does not like people or cannot show character. On the contrary, my point would reaffirm a previous contention: that Shaw tries to get at reality and that his method is movement and his end revelation. If caricature can do this at times, well and good, he will give us caricature: Androcles, Bohun, Brittanus, Alfred Doolittle. Or if the matter requires something more lofty he will give us types like Caesar, John Tanner, or Joan. In each case, the real importance resides in what the character thinks and says and does about reality, not what daydreams and emotions he has that appeal to similar or identical phenomena among the audience.

Shaw will not let us hide. He refuses to let us identify, at least empathetically by means of character. His folk do not act the way we do and the way characters in the movies do. Interestingly, Eliza marries Higgins in the movie of *Pygmalion* but not in the play. No, in the play she most specifically does not marry Higgins, and Shaw goes to some trouble to tell us why she marries the idiotic Freddie instead. Shaw knows that empathy and illusion are dreadful liars and flatterers, and since his business is with art, which never lies because it nothing affirmeth, he wrenches his characters free of stock attitudes, responses, and situations and gives us types acting typically according to the promptings of their lusts and aspirations. This is Jonson, not O'Neill or Tennessee Williams. If at any time Shaw encourages stock responses, it is only that the impending reversal may be the more devastating. See the opening scene of *Arms and the Man*, where Shaw leads the audience into a trap of thinking they are about to witness a lovely romance among high life in Ruritania, then presents a hero who is the symbol of the antiromantic. If Ben Jonson, by the use of humors presents and pillories human lusts in their perverse action, Shaw by the use of the type and the representative pillories those human self-deceptions which have become one grade more effete than lust, which indeed are quite often antihuman because they are based on illusion, flattery, and an unconscious cynicism.

III

Those who are acquainted with the whole of Shaw's drama can see quite readily that the characteristic pattern changes little over the years, though of course the scope widens and the morality gathers more of life into its embrace. "They will not find him changed from him they knew, / Only more sure of all he thought was true." The pattern more and more clearly, from *Widowers' Houses* to *The Apple Cart*, contains further and further ramifications of the ideas of reality and responsibility. We must become our brothers' keepers but first and foremost must turn true keepers of our true selves. This is the essential fact that gives vitality to Shaw's social criticism and theorizing, for although he deals in general and abstract ideas he bases them firmly on a vision of mankind in general and people with all their specific needs. Does this seem paradoxical, that he should present these general types of representative character and yet be so concerned with the lot of the individual? I think not. First, remember that Shaw writes plays, not treatises. And many who go to Shaw to scoff at the doctrine remain to worship the art. You just don't create art out of unreal abstractions, and Shaw himself throughout his work reminds us of this—see notably the preface to *Heartbreak House*. Anyone who tries to see life steadily and see it whole cannot but be abnormally sensitive to the fates of individuals as well as of nations and worlds. In fact, Shaw would say that you cannot suffer for the one and not the other. Thus the play *Heartbreak House*, which Shaw tells us is a vision of a collapsing Europe, finds its locale in the English countryside and has for characters common types of English folk—no cosmic symbols or huge design, only the microcosm. And so it is with the seemingly most frivolous of Shaw plays: always we find that there are overtones and echoes—always the movement outward. In *You Never Can Tell* Shaw says what he says in *Arms and the Man*, in *Saint Joan*, in *Man and Superman*: *nosce te ipsum*, find out what you really are, then be that, in despite of codes and conventional moralism. Yet like any good dramatist he can't simply *say* this; he must show it, and his repertoire for this purpose is immense. The Shavian hero or heroine must come to grips with reality and then put him or her self in tune with it. Is your religion obsolete? Scrap it and get a new one like Undershaft and Barbara in *Major Barbara*. Are you running away from your appointed destiny in love? Turn and embrace it like Tanner in *Man and Superman*. Does your inspiration go directly counter to the abstractions of the powerful and rich? Listen to your voices and not theirs, like Joan in *Saint Joan*. Are you an unlovely person who can't get people to love you? Learn to take such affection as you can get on whatever basis they will give it, like Crampton in *You Never Can Tell*. Do your basic impulses, your essential qualities that make you you, yearn for love and family against doctrine? Give in to them, as Gloria does. If you deny reality you will become at best a buffoon like Broadbent in *John Bull's Other Island* or an unconscious villain like Sir Howard Hallam in *Captain Brassbound's Conversion*. Or perhaps worst of all you may find out too late that you have done great evil for which there is neither redress nor forgiveness, which is the fate of the Chaplain, Stogumber, in *Saint Joan*.

    You Never Can Tell is, God save us, a thing of naught if we are after Great Books, as we so drearily often seem to be. Yet it is more than merely interesting to the scholar or entertaining to the audience, for it contains within its structure the outlines of a pattern found continuously throughout Shaw's work. What he has to say here, lightly and entertainingly, he will say with increased gravity later on, never, it is true, abandoning the comic nor quite embracing the tragic but always getting at the main points of the Shavian argument. Above all, consider this play as part of the large design, of that liturgy for the new religion Shaw felt the theater must supply. Mere entertainment has no place in such a scheme, though sensuous appeal does: as Shaw reminds us, our churches are full of horribly sensuous stimulants that the prude would find outrageous in a theater. Thus, acting on the fullest implications of his suggestion, Shaw creates a comedy that is classic in mode and purpose, spare in its outlines, unequivocal in its condemnation of an unrighteous, hypocritical age. Comedy of this sort is rare, rarer than tragedy and problem-drama, for it demands of the dramatist a perfect balance while he must see deeply into the terrible imbalance of men that we call normality. Thus Shaw calls *Coriolanus* Shakespeare's greatest comedy—he means Classic Comedy—and holds up to laughter in his own work hypocrisies and deceits that make the angels weep. We laugh to save ourselves, not being angels. Had Shaw written tragedies, we would perforce weep with a vengeance. In actual life, of course, there is neither exaltation nor laughter; merely the blind suffering of the unaware child. It is here that Shavian comedy finds its greatest triumph: the almost intolerable inhumanities make us laugh, certainly, but it does not entertain: once we get what Shaw is after, we are stuck with it for good and all and there can be no backing out now. Short of a deliberate hebetude or achieved blindness after the event, we can do only what Shaw demands: do something about it. Religious in this sense Shaw's plays certainly are; no catharsis, no comfortable draining of the soul's passions in a vicarious thrill. Classic comedy like this demands rigor of the mind and of the will. We must laugh and see, understand and grow.

If all this does not show us why *You Never Can Tell* itself is a great play the fault may lie to some extent in the free use of the adjective *great*. One thing emerges unmistakably, however: Shaw is a great moralist, aesthetically and ethically, and that, I take it, is an indispensable attribute of greatness. He would strip *seeming* bare to being, to reality, not just for the fun we find in discomfiture, in a Hobbist enjoyment of the triumph of the ego. No, Shaw firmly believes in an art that instructs and delights, an art that, if it does not actually constitute an appeal to action, a call to arms, most certainly demands a widening of horizons. Thus in *You Never Can Tell* the moral passion of the chief characters conflicts with the human needs: Crampton continually thwarts his own desire for love; Gloria has fallen slave to a mere doctrine, a mere set of opinions, at the expense of her soul's life as Hawthorne would put it. Everyone is brutal to everyone else in the name of all the virtues, just as Cauchon, the Inquisitor, and others cast Joan to the fire with the best motive in the world. "Man cannot bear very much reality," we think as Shaw shows us pattern after pattern wherein creatures writhe in the grip of an actual condition that gives the lie to theory and opinion. For all these things pass and the life force remains. It is our duty to see beyond the convention, the dogma, the unconscious bias (even when these are most unconventional, undogmatic, unbiased). We must, in his phrase, "become capable of metaphysical truth," which entails for man a constant sloughing off of accretions, a stripping away of phenomena. This is the method, the movement; the end is a direct view of humanity and its needs, the revelation.

> VALENTINE: Which of us dare give that man an order again!
> DOLLY: I hope he won't mind my sending him for ginger-beer.
> CRAMPTON (doggedly): While he's a waiter it's his business to wait. If you had treated him as a waiter ought to be treated, he'd have held his tongue.
> DOLLY: What a loss that would have been! Perhaps he'll give us an introduction to his son and let us get into London society.

In the last analysis, only two things count: people and their needs, and a totality of vision. Saint Andrew Undershaft and Saint Joan are equally "saints" in the Shavian canon because equally human in the highest sense. I take this to be sound morality and sound Christianity. Man is less than angel and may not in the temporal order know total grace, yet his very humanity has in its own inferior order not yet found full realization. Shaw demands this— not the impossible or the outright blasphemous but that which man in his nature can do, must do if he is to be fully man. That is what "William" the Waiter tells us, what Caesar tells us, what the Shavian masters of reality insist

on dramatizing for us until we must assent, if only by suspending disbelief for three hours. If the words can become
flesh and dwell among us even for so brief a time, will anyone say this is not great? Great art, great reality, great moral
vision?

Herman Melville's The Encantadas

In America, every artist in fiction or poetry must begin all over again. Ezra Pound said, "Make it new," perhaps—unconsciously one hopes—echoing God: "Behold, I make all things new." In a sense every good or perhaps great writer does start afresh, make a new beginning, which in America is also an end, since no one else can ever do more than imitate, become one of many priests of the cult. Originality may consist merely in cult work-and-ritual, a kind of Yankee whittling or soft-core porn.

Herman Melville was a true original. Being a graduate of nothing much scholastically, he went his ignorant way until, of all things, English literature (mostly poetry and drama) of the Renaissance fell on him like an avalanche. He never recovered, and a good thing. While the Men of Letters were selling their romantic pastiche like good happy merchants, Melville the real romantic was preparing a compound of Sir Thomas Browne, Edmund Spenser, the King James Version and Shakespeare that had nothing in common with the language of Sir Walter Scott or Washington Irving or James Fenimore Cooper, nor with the "poetic diction" of the Boston and New York confectioners. He made up an original style that was part bibliophiliac, part wit-writing, all inventive, the more so for being so derivative. With the instinct of the true genius for surface above depth, he made almost by hand a style and a way of speaking that, while it sometimes fell into bathos and periphrasis, still afforded a great range of tone and feeling. Part of the triumph of Melville's best work derives from that fact: he had the ability to state, as well as to express, to divagate and pause as well as to drive on.

After *Pierre* and the consequent collapse of a shaky reputation, all Melville's hope of making a living by writing died, and much of the confidence in the gift and ambition died too. It was presumably then that Melville somehow determined that he would write his way into and out the other side of what we today would call an existential despair. He was not the last American writer to try that maneuver, and if today we may go along with the existential, up to a point, we know better than to call it despair. Whatever we may choose to call that state of his, Melville lived with it for thirty years, and at the end came *Billy Budd*. In the meantime there were among others the *Piazza Tales*, above all *The Encantadas*, a remarkable series of pieces without parallel in our literature.

After the disastrous *Pierre*, could anyone have expected such a work as this? Here is Melville's personal style, idiom and attitude, at its best and most supple. Here we can see plain the emblematic imagination that he brought to bear on "the fallen world" of nature and men in nature. He had tried allegory in various shapes and sizes; he had, in *Pierre*, tried a mixture of fiction, allegory, satire, and autobiography that satisfied his own craving for meaning as little as it flattered the critics' taste. *The Encantadas* abandons plot, characterization, and drama in favor of description and statement, a kind of "witty" use of overtones of language and sound that combine in the making of emblems of moral, accidental, and natural conduct. He invents here a kind of symbolism that might have fascinated later writers more than that of Poe had they known of Melville's work. The different characters or figures who move through these ten "sketches," exercises in the picturesque, are indeed emblems of conduct, Hart Crane's phrase.

These clinker islands, the Encantadas or Galapagos, burnt-out, forbidding, and sinister, become Melville's emblem of "no world but a fallen one." Supporting life grudgingly if at all, remote, dangerous, and beautiful, they draw the imagination to themselves as their mysterious winds and currents draw resisting vessels. And whether Melville gives us his highly wrought picture of the doubly bereaved, enigmatic Hunilla or a humorous, reverberating image of

the tortoise on the ship's deck unrelentingly pushing against
the mast that bars its single track, always the emblems sink
back into the one source that is Melville's quarrel, not with
God but with himself. The islands that make up the Galapagos group may not be pandemonium, but Melville does
see them as emblematic of nature's absolute indifference,
man's natural depravity, and the gradations and variations
he had himself perceived in his own career as man and
writer. We survive precariously and at the expense of something or someone other, like the castaway sailor of "Sketch
Tenth" who, in an agony of thirst, seizes on the first creature
to hand, and sucks out its life to save his own: "Throwing
himself upon the panting body [of a seal] [he] quaffed at
the living wound; the palpitations of the creature's dying
heart injected life into the drinker." An emblem of conduct
with a vengeance! Again, Hunilla, brought back by her
rescuers to the home whence she and her dead had come,
looks down as she rides slowly away from the beholders,
on "the jointed workings of the beast's armorial cross." Is
the device of the cross merely heraldic? Has Hunilla taken
on the suffering of man in the sense that Christ did? That
she in full humility returns to the city "riding upon a small
grey ass" may strike the reader as perhaps overdoing it a
bit, but it bears out Melville's intention: that Hunilla should
somehow signify absolute suffering and in so doing mark
the consciences and sensibilities of the seamen who have
rescued her. Though she herself is beyond salvation in
this world, may her ordeal have emblematic meaning sufficient to change the lives of those who contemplate those
things?

All these images come out of the writer's concern with
the plight of the self and of the artist in a world that, if not
actively hostile, might better be so. Surely there is a half-
humorous yet wholly serious self-projection in the image
of the tortoise forever butting his head against the mast.
Portrait of the artist as young fool—and as middle-aged
failure. His only recourse: to die there, or to be taken, killed,

and turned into soup, leaving his carapace for a tureen! Gruesome; funny, too, and one might say farfetched if there were not all those exemplars from nature and humanity crowding the pages and all variations on the complex Melvillean theme: how can I go on living in this galley, chained to my oar?

To write great prose is not to broadcast but to speak person to person. The personal style, idiom, and tone make the message. Yet here is a story, if that is what it is, about dead volcanic islands, if that is what they are. In "Sketch First" the imagery of hell or Tartarus—a reference point for Melville—dominates, even as he remembers the softer landscape of the Adirondacks, for he says that he "can hardly resist the feeling that in my time I have indeed slept upon evilly enchanted ground."

Encantadas. Enchantment. The tale is about spells cast by the islands upon men and one woman. And through it all crawls "the ghost of a gigantic tortoise with 'Memento xxx' burning in live letters upon his back." Death in live letters. "Sketch Second" gives us the lives of the tortoises themselves, those creatures that suggest to Melville the horror, venerability, and awe of remote pasts and inscrutable purposes. They become emblems of endurance, instinct with purpose, or intention beyond comprehension. They give Melville nightmares, but that does not keep him from eating them with relish or from making bowls of their shells. And why not? He had known a taste of success only to meet with rejection and failure, but did that mean that he could not rejoice in private—"be secret and exult"? "Sketch Third" takes us to the top of Rock Redondo, a crag often taken at a distance for a ship's sail, the home of thousands of sea birds, all strange, ghostly, alien to the landsman, their somber colors and sinister cries reinforcing the effect of dreariness. And into the midst of this sinister swarm Melville says there comes "a snow-white angelic thing . . . the beauteous bird from its bestirring whistle of musical invocation fitly styled the 'Boatswain's Mate.'" After this

apotheosis, an echo from *Moby Dick*, Melville descends to
the base of the rock where the fish school, prey of the rav-
enous birds: "Poor fish of Redondo . . . you are of the
number of those who inconsiderately trust, while they do
not understand, human nature." A piece of wry self-de-
precation?

The fancy should seem dismal, yet it is immediately
followed in "Sketch Fourth" with one of those pieces of
historical-geographical-navigational fancy so dear to Melville's imagination, and when they are right so delightful to
read for what they are in themselves and for the insight
into the playfulness of one part of Melville's gift. The locale
is still those dismal islands, yet we see them differently.
Melville solemnly gives us the "population" of the island
of Albemarle: men, anteaters, man-haters, lizards, snakes,
spiders, salamanders, devils, making as he says "a clean
total of 11,000,000." A sardonic satisfying of the taste for
"stats." Melville knew well that such figures had for un-
imaginative people an absolute value, were to be loved for
themselves alone. Humor would provide him with a way
to get on with the job, though it might not get a response
from the putative reader.

Thus far man has scarcely appeared in the tale. He ap-
pears, and ironically as buccaneer, in "Sketch Sixth." The
amenities of Barrington Isle Melville describes as not only
"singularly adapted to careening, refitting, refreshing, and
other seaman's purposes," but as a kind of idyllic retreat
where enemies of society relaxed, singly and in company. "I
cannot," says Melville, "avoid the thought that it is hard
to impute the construction of these romantic seats to any
other motive than one of pure peacefulness and kindly fel-
lowship with nature." Someone had built these rustic stone
seats with views commanding sea and islands. Who else
but these Gilbertian buccaneers: Melville surely wants us
to draw the conclusion not only that it takes all kinds, but
that some buccaneers are more virtuous than "honest" men.
The sketch ends with an extension of the thought expressed

in "Sketch Third," that of the incomprehensibility of human nature: "Among these adventurers were some gentlemanly, companionable souls, capable of genuine tranquillity and virtue." Perhaps *tranquillity* is the startling, pivotal word. And its irony shows plain in the sketch that follows, in which we see a war of men against dogs and against their fellow men. The captain warns his third mate not to think the light that shows from the island is a signal from helpless, shipwrecked men: it is a false light set by wreckers: "It tempts no wise man to pull off and see what's the matter, but bids him steer small and keep offshore."

Not for Melville the illusion that mere man can cure or shun evil by ignoring its existence. This captain is no Captain Delano; he knows that wickedness is no Calvinist fancy: "Brace up, Mr. Mate, and keep the light astern." But this vessel is a merchant vessel, not *Indomitable*; there are no articles of war to condemn her to go in harm's way. Claggart cannot be left astern, as the murderous tyranny of the Dog King may be in this case. Authority must have its Claggarts, and of course the King will have other recruits. In every case there is both murderer and murderee, as Edmund Pearson says. Melville puzzles over it again and again: how it is that bad can be so good, good so dumb, helpless, almost consenting? In "Sketch Eighth," the story of "Norfolk Isle and the Chola Widow," we have the tale near to the kind of sentimental "tears and flapdoodle" that in part drove Melville out of the league. It is the kind of thing Hawthorne could manage with great success; his toughness of mind would not let the sentiments "bother him none," as the fisherman said to the tourist about the sunset. It bothered Melville. Lacking the ability to create character, he made emblems, and Hunilla, the Chola widow, is too afflicted and bereaved for Melville to be able to treat her emblematically. It may be that the sketch has a trace of weakness on this score. Perhaps those dogs she must leave behind, after we have been treated to the Dog King, seem too much. Hawthorne wouldn't have done that, but Hawthorne knew

women a lot better and is perhaps the only American novelist who can create believable female characters. I don't
think Melville felt that deeply for Hunilla, but he did feel
for what she stood for: "nature's pride subduing nature's
torture."

To whatever degree Melville may have allowed sentimentalities to infect his true feeling toward Hunilla, there
is no false note in the almost burlesque comedy of Oberlus,
the murderous "hermit" of Hood's Isle, an outcast who has
all the qualities of a small-town capitalist, from false friendship to savagery. He is the finest kind of emblem, digging
among his clinkers with his back turned on his interlocutor,
at a loss whether to seal a bargain or a fate. He is the true
misanthrope. Not content to avoid men, he must force himself and his sinister habits on the innocent seamen who
come to him for supplies. His instinct is murderous and destructive, in strong contrast to the buccaneers whose natures
are free and open, and who, though guilty of a bit of
violence and rapine here and there, run an honest business
in their way and are the best of company. Oberlus is cursed
by God and a bad temper. Melville sees him as a figure of
fun, the devil not so much sick as psychotic.

The Encantadas is a fine introduction to the best of
Melville's work. If only he could have written it instead
of *Pierre*! Most people are not Melville nuts or scholars.
Only a mother (whose?) could love Pierre or *Pierre*—except
in parts, as the curate said of the egg. Melville wrote that
obligatory novel when and as he had to, and we know the
price he paid for the tactical error. If there is not the kind
of "topgallant delight" in these sketches that is in *Moby
Dick*, there is all the pleasure, humor, and artistry—with
a touch of pathos—of the main deck. It is art, a thing fully
made for pleasure, reflection, and remembering.

Romance of the Rose:
John Peale Bishop and Phelps Putnam

The crisis that beset the poetic mind in the period of the "aesthetic revolution" between let us say the 1890s and the 1930s manifested itself in a number of ways, and perhaps the most exciting yet destructive of those ways was the symbolic, a phenomenon that never became a movement but nevertheless stamped the poetic temper of the time. It became a way of perceiving and making that grew more barbarous with its excess. Perhaps it did indeed begin in America with Poe, but it came back home with a vengeance, fully empowered by Baudelaire, *les symbolistes*—indeed by a whole aesthetic movement which we dub the Decadence or impressionism or a number of offshoots of Pound's imagism before it turned into Amygism. The isolation of the physical object and the experience of it, the free association of its clusters of private feeling and memory: that set the thing going. Afterward, all things of a symbolistic nature were possible. But the key to it, or rather, the keys, are solipsism and ritualism. Whether we talk of Oscar Wilde or Hart Crane or Rimbaud, we come to the hedonistic self under aesthetic pressure and the exfoliating or ramifying from a single source that object and the sense of it which compose the symbol. Rose, Tower, Sea, River, Vessel—a few such "structures" sum up part of the postromantic sensibility in its grand design to make the single psyche prevail over essence and existence, to turn all of life into a single, constantly expanding work of art.

That, nowadays, comes to seem more and more what the poets we have found most "interesting" seemed to have attempted, knowingly or not. Rimbaud's drunken boat, Crane's wine and jazz records, Putnam's "long debauchery" have this in common: they seek to isolate and freeze the random element in the universe, and of course in trying to bring their gaze into focus upon that element they repel it. But symbolism can never be an aesthetic position or a poetic strategy: it is purely phenomenal and depends for its rare valid occurrences in certain poems upon specific coincidences of the man and the moment of his insertion of himself, all calculatedly, into the atomistic flux or stream that constitutes his aesthetic sense of particular experiences. Obscurantism is the vice of the method; splendor and a stretching of the fancy its virtues. Like all romantic art, symbolism has a powerful infusion of the homeopathic. Seemingly unlike things compose into likeness within the whole that the entire poem seeks to make of its expanding elements. The aim is to find an ultimate synthesis among contraries by making impossible conjunctions of disparate elements. Repetitive, flowing, incantatory, it tends to be a poetry of great rational control over deliberately irration-alized elements. Crane's "The Broken Tower" surely shows the method at its best, as his "At Melville's Tomb" displays the mechanical, destructive, and obscurantist elements that always threaten a symbolist work. Those spirits summoned from the vasty deep are sometimes—often—either low comics or plastic monsters.

It was this poetic world that Phelps Putnam chose, or which chose him. To make of one's own personal expe-rience—friends, loves, the world of sacramental play—all these were to be ritualized and made into a kind of pagan cult, in which one celebrated the "rose" of sensuality with such intensity that all impurities were burned away and the refined essence remained: the poem itself. Putnam perhaps felt that in a time barren of myth and ritual, poetry had to make them again from scratch. Out of the experience of his brief poetic life he made another All-American try at the great white goal or whale. So did Hart Crane, with better luck, bad as that was. Of John Peale Bishop one can say only that he looked into that chaos and tried to win to his vision on other terms, those of the epic ironist who sees in advance what the event means and, knowing, sets it down without hope or fear.

Romance. Conradian word. Taking different forms for different men and literary occasions and temperaments, it ruled the age. Still does perhaps. Looking at the back files of *The New Republic*, in search of material for this essay, I came upon the name Howard Coxe, my uncle, Princeton, class of 1920, a romantic figure of my youth. He once saw, if not Shelley, certainly Scott and Hem and so many others plain. Had he not done his time working for the Paris *Herald*? done the places that had to be done? And for his sins he got tuberculosis, romantic disease enough in fable and fiction, but scarcely in fact. But I saw him as romantic indeed—I was about twenty when I found out what he had done and who he was, more or less. I remember seeing him just before he went to Saranac to die, as it turned out, bedridden in his little house above the Hudson at Sniden's Landing. He died at forty, a disappointed man of great charm, wit, and intelligence whose ambition to become a great or perhaps only good novelist he had seen fade and fail, as though the tuberculosis were its somatic counterpart.

Romance. Phelps Putnam would try, by an effort of unaided will, to turn his own youthful friendships, experience, reading, and affections into a fable, almost a legend, that could carry a self-perpetuating myth. Seeing all these things, himself included, as larger than life, he brought youth's passionate melancholy and capacity for romantic melodrama (with oneself as hero of course) to bear on what can properly be described as typical college-boy experiences, hoping to charge them with imaginative power. Yeats, one thinks—or perhaps Shelley? Not quite. Both Putnam and John Bishop, like so many of their contemporaries and rivals, were Princeton, Yale, or Harvard men, and indeed products of fashionable eastern prep schools. Interesting to note that among the novelists, neither Faulkner nor Hemingway went beyond high school, and that Hart Crane, whose name must surely crop up in any talk of these men and times may justly be said to have had no education at all. It did not help him any more than Skull and Bones helped Putnam. But what makes so much of that "lost" generation so exciting to us today, so romantic and so doomed (Faulknerian word) is the spell their very legends cast of romance, of great original promise bravely, even exhilaratingly, made but not really kept.

Putnam's gift seemed to die almost imperceptibly, though he came to know it, while he himself died, not fast enough one feels, of a horrible asthma. The first poems he published—I found one of them in *The New Republic* of June 6, 1923—were inevitably about Yale College—they called them colleges in those days—and graduation therefrom. Ceremony. An end. Possibly a new beginning. For Putnam the past, his personal past, formed the basis of his personal mythology which he attempted to create as the groundwork and substance of his poetry, much as Faulkner was beginning to do at the same time and as Hart Crane had already done in a few poems: *The White Buildings* came out in 1926. Allen Tate was not far from that Mediterranean locus classicus that would soon take form from his poetic mythos. Yet with a difference in each case; and every case, for all the difficulty and perhaps horror with which each was beset, produced better, more powerful work than did Putnam. Why?

Is the question proper or valid? Maybe, if we look at what Putnam actually brought to his task—looking, be it said with humility and with gratitude for those things well done and in some awe of the willingness to pay the price. First, it seems to me that Putnam lacked the intellectual resources of the other men. Hemingway may have affected the "mucker pose" and so on, Crane was "uneducated" though he had read widely, but Putnam, unliterary as he seems to have been, had far less to draw on. I take it as axiomatic that a writer must be an avid reader, or have been one some time in his career, preferably early; he needs that fat to live off. Putnam did not really have it and as a result (this is pure conjecture) he had to feed his imagination on personal events which lacked resonance because he could not live vicariously in words and books as well as in the actual. And of course the asthma—and the drink, which beginning as the symbolist's "dérèglement de tous les sens" ended as painkiller. Putnam saw his gift fade from him, but it did not go until after he had written at least three poems of extraordinary power, poems unmistakably his and made to last: "Ballad of A Strange Thing," "Hasbrouck and the Rose," and "Hymn to Chance," the first from his first volume, *Trinc*, and the others from its successor, *The Five Seasons*.

The "exantlation" that takes place reminds strongly of Yeats but the rhetoric is not Yeatsian, nor the locations and ambiences of the poems anything but American, the America of Connecticut farmland and Springfield, Massachusetts. Walt Whitman's influence may show here, but again, not in the rhetoric, certainly not in the cadences. Putnam was a highly "conventional" metricist. But what happens in, to begin with, the "Ballad of A Strange Thing" shows that Putnam had the power to start conversationally, then suddenly send it up and out into another dimension, partly by rhetorical, partly by thematic, means. At the close of the poem, we as readers are brought back to the actual, not so much changed as hung over: we have felt the true intoxication, then must return to sobriety "more / Dull and baffled than before." And that is the final line of the poem.

Now the most, or at any rate not the least, remarkable quality of the poem is its technical control: something that would seem to cry out for expressive, if not imitative, form. The seemingly random appearance of the magical Jack Chance, the "dozen foolish farmers" with their hard cider, the wild pagan tale that Jack tells: one feels that tone and control could readily go bad, turn excessive, either à la Swinburne or in the twenties mode, à la *Jurgen*. Putnam here has perfected just that element of style for which he has often been faulted: language in movement, meter as opposed to cadence. Even the name, Jack Chance, works perfectly here, as the Bill Williams of Putnam's homemade myth does not. Few modern American poems—E. A. Robinson's "Isaac and Archibald" is one—mingle local, homegrown, and mythical, almost "universal," elements with personal themes from the poet's own work and experience. Yvor Winters complained that Yeats spent a good deal of time trying to inflate the importance of his perfectly ordinary friends by name-dropping and myth-mongering. Well, Putnam does it here, and for the best of reasons: for a moment, an eternal one, those friends and that place become myth, the real thing, and with no sense of strain, of trying to push the subject up to a higher level than our imagination is under the circumstances willing to climb—as, for example, in a poem as impressive as "On the Death of Major Robert Gregory," where the periphrastic concluding stanza may just not succeed, or in "Among Schoolchildren," the sudden wrench from stanza one to two may not reach the plane it must if the poem is to have full effect. In the "Ballad" the personal style, the rapid and deft metric and the perfect harmony of near-formal and near-colloquial diction make us wholly prepared for Jack Chance's marvelous tale, just as it all works equally well to take us down from that height to the reality of a mythless New England where no marvels are.

These techniques work again in "Hasbrouck and the Rose" though the latter poem is far shorter and it may be that the conclusion does not, in its calculated banality, bring us back to the world unmythed and desolate in the resonating manner Putnam evidently intended. But the poem makes of tone and technique a strategic triumph, on a lesser scale from that of the "Ballad." Again, no expressive or imitative form. If there are echoes here, perhaps of Stevens's "The Worms at Heaven's Gate," it might be said, why not echoes in the latter of the former? The poem is full of echoes and is meant to be; Putnam is, after all, a romantic. He had a firm belief, for a while, that anything could happen, even in New England.

And in a sense, happen it did, in the person of John Peale Bishop, whose very existence as man and poet displays all the anomalies of the poet in America; perhaps indeed in the modern western world. He was not, to begin with, like Putnam a kind of child of nature and impulse: on the contrary, a man of very complex and subtle quality whose mixed southern and New England ancestry and upbringing, near-aristocratic lineage, and American-Latinate language and attitudes seem to me to characterize the typical modern American poet of real quality. That is to say, he is a contradiction; he belongs but not quite; he is of his time and place and station but not fully. In other words, he is the artist according to Thomas Mann, as most fully expressed in "Tonio Kroger": the artist as child of the time yet of another time as well, who can only try to "get used to not getting used," as Mann says of his Hans Castorp. Allen Tate, in his introduction to Bishop's *Selected Poems*, makes a point of this uncomfortable state when he declares that Bishop, coming as he did at a time of the collapse of "Rome" (read the United States), comes at the precise moment of truth for the poet: "this moment of collapse produces the aesthetic vision: visual perception is restored to the symbolic image; and this is the moment of aesthetic consciousness."

The argument is the same as that elaborated more fully in Tate's essay on that other remarkable creature caught between worlds, Emily Dickinson; we can perhaps wish to press the point further and apply it to all the poets of America, excluding of course the Sons of Walt. But I think in this case it is to the poets of the South—the Fugitives and their kin—to whom we must look: Donald Davidson, Allen Tate, John Crowe Ransom (a little), some of Robert Penn Warren, specifically in the case of his poem "Court Martial." The Fugitives, and Bishop has affinities to them, have to one degree or another the power to restore us to our Mediterranean past, in the literature and the myth, as well as at moments to the roots of the Christianity that haunts the work of all these poets. Bishop, it seems to me, must have known and valued Davidson's "Sanctuary" and other poems as well. There are occasions in his work when we think not so much of Tate or Davidson or Ransom (who is in any case too "eccentric" for the purpose) as of a certain body of thought and belief, a cultural heritage and commitment that the individual poems and poets exist to assert or defend. In the 1970s one might possibly wonder if those "reactionary essays" (Tate's phrase) may not be after all more potent than we had thought. John Bishop was no mere postromantic longing for the dear dead halcyon days: he was no Scholar-Gypsy, but a man who fought off a culture, if that's the word, in order to achieve "the moment of aesthetic con-sciousness." His way was not Hart Crane's nor Putnam's; those were the ways of Rimbaud, and they did not ultimately work, being deadly, and usable up to the age of twenty only! Derangement can certainly be achieved: that requires no fur-ther proof. But does it succeed? Does it exact more than it ever gave? Can one go on indefinitely creating chaos hoping to make an order from it?

Homeopathic dosages were not for Bishop: he wanted form, wanted to be able to say, *Civis Romanus sum*: or at least, I wish I were. His creed, or part of it, is stated most personally in his poem to Edmund Wilson, "No More the Senator." Roman *virtus* alone can and should prop a man in these bad days, he tells his friend. In "Speaking of Poetry," there is the elaborated analogy of aesthetic tenor: the marriage of Desdemona to Othello as the symbol of what a work of art must accomplish: "The ceremony must be found / That will wed Desdemona to the huge Moor." Ceremony, ritual, virtue, power. All these must exist in concert and in alliance with sensibility, delicacy, grace. It would seem that Bishop could not rest in the sterile condi-tion of the anathematist; it was not enough to curse god and die; one had to put one's money where one's mouth was and work it out in the poetry or in the life. In his analogical-symbolic way, Bishop achieves that difficult victory in two poems, "The Return" and "Perspectives Are Precipices."

The latter poem is a quiet marvel of technical proficiency. Nowadays one is expected to apologize for that and go on into the sincerity and sloppy feeling of it all—which is of course just what Bishop did not want: he wanted to marry effete Desdemona to the "barbarous" Othello, in art as well as in action and feeling. "Perspectives" uses the old Bluebeard tale, the old question-and-answer, to set, indeed to dramatize, a surreal landscape in which there is "a man who goes / Dragging a shadow by its toes." The clipped epigrammatic couplets, the dramatic final vision of the man "gone . . . into the sun" not only suggest certain surrealist art but brings the reader into the world of total desert. "I saw a man but he is gone / His shadow gone into the sun." The off-rhyme, the only one in the poem, strikes with a dead sound. No moralizing, no emotive language, no exhortation. The poem exists in an atmosphere of arid rigor —and we know that the same scene reenacts itself forever, always receding, always present.

Control and power. The use of small means to gain large ends. The American Roman poets of this school had a healthy distrust of romantic rhetoric and its cult of "derangement," as well as of its populist-bardic expansiveness. Yet their own sensibility was romantic, European, Mediterranean as well as southern American, local as well as civilized. Bishop tells in "The Return" of the twilight and death of the gods, of the failure first of faith, lastly of life. Have we a kind of *Waste Land*? Is this another in the long series of doom-gatherings à la Robinson Jeffers? Because Bishop has his Roman history and its long exemplary drama for his locus, he can use the shorthand of image and symbol in a compressed elliptical way that shuns the imitative form and capriciousness that mar *The Waste Land*. He concentrates, and rather than resort to the imitative or indeed the expressive, compresses his effects in the telling image, symbol, or event. Thus, "vultures starved"; "it was the young whose child did not survive"; "the sea unfurled." As in "Perspectives," every phrase must count, by itself and as part of a whole. It is not necessary, to show disaster, to be disastrous, nor in order to express death, to die on the page. "The ceremony must be found."

Yeats thought he had found it, dragged it "lock stock and barrel / Out of his bitter soul." Put Putnam knew better; he knew that the Rose, great symbol since the Middle Ages of incarnation and passion, of love, honor, and their opposites, had perished. In "Hasbrouck and the Rose," all of the meanings of the Rose as ceremony and its burden reach a culmination and an end in a cheap hotel room: "In Springfield, Massachusetts I devoured the rose" Hasbrouck declares. And again, finally: "I have eaten it . . . / There is no rose." The poets have seen the world devour its own meaning: "the sad rose of all the world," in Yeats's phrase. As Christian, sexual, and mystical nexus, it simply disappeared into "the guts of the living" and presumably persists only as excrement.

The ceremony had been found, efficacious for one set of circumstances, but the romantic attempt to epitomize "the whole combustible world in one small room," again as Yeats put it, was as doomed as Yeats knew it to be, and as Bishop knew it. Crane proved it by his death, a long day's dying and it still goes on. Phelps Putnam and John Peale Bishop found that momentary stay against confusion in a few poems; in Bishop's case, more than two or three. The poets of our own contemporaneity have done no more; indeed, it may be that in these matters, More swiftly becomes Less. Putnam lacked mind, the contemplative brooding spirit informed by experience and that vicarious life books hold. Bishop apparently thought and thought well, as poet and man, with informed weight behind that thought: he could see beyond and find putative states of being and thinking that eluded Putnam and that Hart Crane could yearn for but for which he could not find the ceremonial evocation to call them to life—except in his last and perhaps greatest, certainly most fully orchestrated, poem, "The Broken Tower." Yet it remained for Allen Tate, in "The Mediterranean," to give to the whole theme its fullest, gravest, and most Vergilian expression. The ceremony, when it is found in a given case, brings mind as well as spirit and belief to bear on a metaphysical state that has ceased to be merely personal—Eliot's "condition of complete simplicity." The miracle is that we have these poems by Putnam and Bishop written out of the heart of the anguish. What that involved in the way of making something out of next to nothing the next generation of poets has discovered, to its cost.

After Words

What is literary criticism for? or about? Who, as they say, needs it? Well, as Lear puts it, "Allow not nature more than nature needs. / Man's life's as cheap as beast's." Or cheaper. Why should anyone waste time and words on something that cannot begin to solve our problems? Can literary chatter, however fancy, *do* anything to help us in our parlous state? Forget the questions: give us the answers.

In the beginning was the Word. Don't argue: the Word means the Incarnate Logos, whatever that means. All literary argument, discussion, shop talk, and speculation take for granted the fact that none of it makes any difference—unless you happen to need and like that kind of thing. The Word can be made flesh, can dwell among us. It can also become a late-night talkshow, or any private or corporate pack of lies. Literary criticism has one sole function, in this context: to find within all those words, the Word, and to cut away from a given work or body of work the excrescences that time and abuse and neglect and incomprehension have grafted upon it. Our ideal critic can shed more light in a generous spirit of shared vision—intense, indeed partial, but in the interest of the works he would bring home to us, to our wider knowledge. He would teach us not only how, but what, to read, and to learn a proper contempt for the fake and shoddy.

Can a single critic do all that? No. But he should try and in the trying encourage others to do likewise—to begin again to read, to judge, to enjoy. When there is no criticism there is no literature. Interestingly, even the pop arts share this illness, but that's another and sillier story. Here and now the question is, how do I know what I mean till I and another see what I say? As true for the poet as the critic, and we have to begin with the simple, sad assertion: there is no audience. Well, of course in this country there never has been, and many a man has written anguished prose dedicated to the castigation of American middle-class readers, television, movies and so on, but never doing more than relieving his own feelings, if that—certainly not ours. Why all this nonsense?

Let us begin. First, good literature, high literature never did, does not, never will make you better, wiser, richer, cuter or more of anything except perhaps unhappy. Call it Afflicted with Divine Discontent if that makes you feel better, or worse, according to choice. The fact remains that Auden was not just being perverse when he said "poetry makes nothing happen," and we all know that poets are an obnoxious lot, on the whole; fiction writers, bores. All of them raving egomaniacs and so on. Indeed, many of them are just like people—though what difference it makes to anyone who is not hopelessly involved with one or another of these monsters is the point: we want our writers to be TV Personalities, only more foul and "tragic." TV performers are not suicidal, whereas with any luck your favorite switch-hitting poet may take the big dive any day, and then think of all the opportunities for knocked-out elegy and sad self-centered reflections on the poet as Christ taking our sins upon himself, or as the Bearer of the Wound and the Bow. All of this in Poetry, so to speak. The truth is that we have managed once again the middle-class miracle: transferred epithet or mixed metaphor. Set up a model of reality, then take it for reality itself. Call it by a general or categorical name to put it beyond the reach of discussion, analysis, contemplation.

Book reviewing. Breaking into print. Selling out to anyone not so much as interested. Trying to please. Apart from the venality and sycophancy of it all, one wants to know: What does all this corruption and ignorance mean? Nothing. Most people do not read because they do not associate pleasure or exaltation with reading; hence they do not know how to read and will not try to learn lest in the learning they discover a liking, perhaps a passion, for something that can only mean trouble and no money. Which is not to say that real readers are nice. Only that they are more interesting to be with, if one happens to be a reader oneself. Perhaps Robert Graves is right after all, whether or not one likes his poetry: poets should live like the inhabitants of Tierra del Fuego where everyone lives by taking in everyone else's laundry. A bit ingrown, but nowhere else in the world is laundry done so well.

Poetry can start only in the mind and imagination of a genius. Talent is nothing, talent anyone can acquire by means of a couple of books, ambition, and an act of attention. Poetic genius can be badly—fatally—flawed, but will show itself nonetheless. It is entirely random, and except under exceptional circumstances, irresponsible. Talent can be brash, or slavish, but it never transcends the mode it adopts in any given instance. It does not imitate, it mocks or chatters. "Mere" genius can be so badly served by ignorance, psychosis, or despair that actual or ritual suicide results. No genius "sells out" in the ordinary venal senses: the gift goes bad because a combination of the social and economic pressures and what used to be called "weakness of character" perverts its spirit. But the real literary genius can indeed sell out, upon occasion, then buy back in: the demon, or daemon, never lets him alone. It is a true possession that may indeed be, often is, imitated in the marketplace. And many a true poet is haunted all his life by the little voice that whispers, Do you really have it? Did you just make the whole thing up? Illusion both kills and sustains. It is a question of which is to come first.

No one knows what he wants until he has found it and then he doesn't. We used to be told that movies had it all. Then it was TV. Remember Marshall Whatsisname? For all he knows or I know, it may even be true. But anyone who has lived in the world of books as well as in what we lightly call our world, knows that a taste or capacity for good literature, particularly poetry, is as random, unexpected and uncanny as genius itself; just as illiteracy, for all that illiterate sociologists and upgraded gym teachers may say, very frequently is a condition pandemic in all societies. Literary texts frighten, disturb, subvert, puzzle, and apparently enrage most people. They simply cannot associate pleasure with what neither profits nor scratches an itch. And it is, after all, difficult to become a prominent lawyer, medicine man or drug king: it takes hard work and concentration, at least for a few years. But anyone can make it to the top in the literary league if he learns the system and "abandons his mind to it." Nothing to do with art, everything to do with politics. A real *work* of literature, the poem nearly anonymous, begins in the visible world, and however far it goes, returns again—"true to the kindred points of Heaven and Home."